P9-DVA-292

THE NEW TESTAMENT YOU NEVER KNEW

EXPLORING THE CONTEXT, PURPOSE, AND MEANING OF THE STORY OF GOD

STUDY GUIDE | EIGHT SESSIONS

N.T. WRIGHT AND MICHAEL F. BIRD

WITH KEVIN AND SHERRY HARNEY

 **ZONDERVAN**®

ZONDERVAN

The New Testament You Never Knew Study Guide
Copyright © 2019 by N. T. Wright and Michael F. Bird

This title is also available as a Zondervan ebook.

Requests for information should be addressed to:
Zondervan, 3900 Sparks Dr., SE, Grand Rapids, MI 49546

ISBN 978-0-310-08526-3 (softcover)

ISBN 978-0-310-08527-0 (ebook)

Interior imagery: Inmagine, Planet Art, Shutterstock, Zondervan
Interior design: Kait Lamphere

First Printing November 2018 / Printed in the United States of America

CONTENTS

INTRODUCTION

EYE-OPENING MOMENTS

We all have moments that shock us. Something was right there in front of us, but we simply did not see it. We did not understand. We just never noticed. Then, in a flash—at the snap of a finger, at the speed of thought—we understand. We get it!

Our eyes snap open.

Many young women and men have an eye-opening moment when they bring their first newborn home from the hospital. After a few days of diapers, sleep deprivation, and perpetual feeding, the reality hits them. *My parents did this for me! They changed a thousand diapers. They cared for me through countless sleepless nights. Mom and Dad provided for me in ways I never really knew . . . until this moment.*

Some people experience such sobering moments of clarity when they try a new food. They knew a certain food was there all along. Other people talked about it. They just never tried it. But then someone offers it to them for the first time, and their taste buds cry out, *Sushi is delicious! How could I have missed it?* Or, *Coffee is intoxicating! Why did I say no so many times through the years?* Or, *Baklava is glorious! How did I not know about this?*

Many people have likewise heard sermons from the New Testament but have never had their eyes opened to the power of those words. They have heard passages quoted from the New Testament but never realized how those seemingly random fragments fit together to tell a glorious and eternity-impacting story. They might have read portions of the New Testament, or even the entire text of those twenty-seven books, but the lights have never switched on.

This eight-week study is designed to help you have one of these eye-opening moments. There is more in the New Testament than you imagine. There are truths you may have overlooked and lessons that might have slipped by. But if you will open your heart and mind, the King of all kings is ready to awaken your imagination. He is waiting to speak and teach the truth to you. The Spirit of the Living God is longing to whisper fresh truth into your ears.

The kingdom of God is closer than you think. The books of the New Testament have been given to unfold the story of God's love, grace, and truth. If you are ready, God is prepared to give you an epiphany, a revelation, and a fresh insight.

There are things about the New Testament that *you never knew.* It is time to have your eyes opened. Brace yourself . . . God is near and ready to move!

HOW TO USE
THIS GUIDE

G et ready for an adventure! Over the course of the next eight weeks, your hosts, N.T. Wright and Michael F. Bird, are going to lead you on a unique journey to the lands where Jesus taught and ministered, the apostle Paul traveled and preached, and the early church took root before exploding throughout the Roman Empire. As they guide you step by step in this journey, you will get to know more about the story *behind* the New Testament, how it came to be written, why it was written . . . and what it means to your life today.

This study is designed to be experienced as a home Bible study, Sunday school class, or other small-group setting. Ultimately, the idea is not just for you to gain knowledge but also to experience life transformation, grow in relationship with others, and apply what you learn to your life. And what better way to do that than surrounded by a group of friends?

Each session in this study guide includes opening "Talk About It" questions, video teaching notes, group discussion questions, and closing prayer suggestions. As a group, you will watch the video and then use the video notes and questions to engage with the topic. Note that you have complete freedom as to how to best use these elements to meet the needs of your group. Again, the goal is experiencing life change, not just "covering the material."

To get the most out of your group experience, keep the following two points in mind. First, remember the real growth in this study will happen during your small-group time. This is where you will process the content of the teaching for the week, ask questions, and learn from others as you hear what God is doing in their lives. For this reason, it is important for you to be fully committed to the group and attend each session so you can build trust and rapport with the other members. If you choose to only "go through the motions," or if you refrain from participating, there is a lesser chance you will find what you're looking for during this study.

Second, make sure your small group is a place where people can share, learn about God, and build intimacy and friendship with one another. Seek to make your group a "safe place" by being honest about your thoughts and feelings and listening carefully to everyone else's opinion. Resist the temptation to "fix" a problem someone might be having or to correct his or her theology, as that's not the purpose of your small-group time. (Note that if you are a group leader, there are additional instructions and resources provided in the back of this study guide to help you lead a productive discussion group.)

Following your group time, you can reflect on the material you've covered by engaging in any or all of the between-sessions activities. For each session, you may wish to complete the personal study all in one sitting or spread it out over a few days (for example, working on it a half-hour a day on different days that week). If you are unable to finish—or even start—your personal study, be sure to still attend the group study video session. You are still wanted and welcome at the group even if you don't have your "homework" done.

It's not a coincidence or accident that you have chosen to participate in this journey! God has great things in store for you, and as you travel the lands of the New Testament during the next eight weeks, he will reveal himself to you in ways you might not expect. So be open to what he is doing in your life . . . as you learn more about *The New Testament You Never Knew*.

Of Note

The quotations and text boxes in this study guide are from *The New Testament You Never Knew Video Study* by N.T. Wright and Michael F. Bird. All other resources, including the small-group questions, session introductions, prayer direction, and between-sessions materials, were written by Kevin and Sherry Harney in collaboration with N.T. Wright and Michael F. Bird.

THE BOOKS OF THE NEW TESTAMENT

Anyone who picks up the New Testament will find, if they give it a chance, that it is one of the most explosive books ever written.

N.T. WRIGHT

INTRODUCTION

There is a massive difference between being familiar with something and understanding it. Having an acquaintance and building a deep friendship are radically different experiences. Flying on a plane and being an aeronautical mechanic are not the same thing!

In the same way, when it comes to the New Testament, many of us are familiar with it. We have an "acquaintance" kind of relationship with this ancient collection of twenty-seven books. But the real question is . . . *do we know and understand the New Testament?*

Imagine you have gone to the same doctor for more than twenty years. You know his name and can predict how he will be dressed (he always wears a long white coat that buttons in the front). You have a good sense of his interests. He likes to ask questions about your health, eating habits, and exercise disciplines. You could certainly identify your doctor in a crowd. He is caring and compassionate and is quick to ask questions about you.

After twenty years, you are confident you know your doctor.

Then one day, you go to a dinner party with friends and are delighted to discover your doctor is also there. As you listen to him throughout the evening, you are amazed to learn all sorts of new things about this man you thought you knew. For one, he has a wife—which had never really crossed your mind. He also has two sons and is clearly fond of them. Later, in a quieter conversation with a few people, you also discover he had a daughter who died when she was only eighteen months old. As he describes the loss, you realize the experience was more than two decades ago, but there is still real pain behind his eyes and in his heart.

During the course of the evening, you have learned your doctor is far more complex, interesting, and real than you had ever imagined. This new context and interaction has opened your eyes and heart to a whole new person you now see in a completely different light. You realize that while you *knew* your doctor, you never *really knew* your doctor.

Perhaps you know the New Testament at the same level you know your doctor. You've interacted with it here and there. You've heard your pastor use it in sermons at church. You've read a few passages here and there. Maybe you have even read the *entire* Bible. But you don't really know it personally . . . or the incredible story that it has to tell.

Over the next eight weeks, your hosts N.T. Wright and Michael F. Bird will invite you to "get out of the office" and get to know the real story behind the New Testament. The table is set. The agenda is clear. It's time to enter into a deeper understanding of the New Testament than you have ever experienced before.

TALK ABOUT IT

Welcome to the first session of *The New Testament You Never Knew*. If you or any of your group members do not know one another, take a few minutes to introduce yourselves. Then, to get things started, discuss one of the following questions:

- Think about a relationship you've had where you *thought* you knew the person, but in a different setting, you saw that person in a completely different light. What was the experience? What did you learn?

—*or*—

- How were you introduced to the New Testament? What do you hope to learn about the New Testament in this study that you did not know before?

The Bible
The Bible is a collection of sixty-six books. They are broken into two parts. The Old Testament has thirty-nine books and the New Testament has twenty-seven books. The Old Testament was originally written in Hebrew and the New testament in Greek. These books were written by a wide variety of people over a wide expanse of time. Anyone who picks up the New Testament will find, if they give it a chance, that it is one of the most explosive books ever written.

VIDEO TEACHING NOTES

Play the video segment for session one. As you watch, use the space provided to collect your thoughts and make some notes about the New Testament that are new and fresh for you.

The Gospels and Acts

Matthew, Mark, and Luke: three similar accounts of Jesus' life, death, and resurrection

The Gospel of John: a unique look at Jesus

Acts: the apostles, early church, and spread of the gospel

The Letters of Paul

What we know about Paul and what he is writing about in his letters

The Apostle Paul

In the Greek, the letters that Paul wrote are fairly brief—about 150 pages. This is much less text than the letters written by Cicero about a hundred years earlier or the letters of Seneca. We don't know when Paul was born. He was most likely a fairly young man when Jesus was crucified and raised from the dead. What we do know is that when we first encounter Saul (later named Paul) in the book of Acts, he is a hot and fiery persecutor of the early Christians. He hated the idea of people following the crucified would-be Messiah. He saw Jesus as a danger to the traditions of Israel, destructive to their laws, and a threat to the temple that they loved. Paul was part of a Jewish sect called the Pharisees and he was committed to do all he could to stamp out the followers of Jesus.

The General Letters

Hebrews: Jesus is better

James: faith without works is dead

Jude: beware of false teachers

1 and 2 Peter: remember who you are and guard your faith

1, 2, and 3 John: love God, love others, and uphold the truth

The Book of Revelation

How we should read the book of Revelation

Where Did the New Testament Come From?

The Bible did not fall from the sky, written in "Ye Olde English" with the words of Jesus in red print. It came through a particular process— through the story and struggles of the early church. The Holy Spirit drew it together from the diaries they were keeping, the sermons they were preaching, the problems they were facing and seeking to solve, and the faith they were striving to live out each day.

GROUP DISCUSSION

Take a few minutes to discuss what you just watched and explore these concepts together.

1. In what ways could we consider the writings of the New Testament "explosive" and "powerful"? How have you experienced this power unleashed in your own life through the teachings contained in the New Testament?

2. Jesus and the early Christians believed that he was the place that heaven and earth actually meet and come together. If you believe this is true, how is Jesus the place that heaven and earth intersect? What difference does it make if this is true?

3. Read the following passages from the beginning of the four Gospels:

> The book of the family tree of Jesus the Messiah, the son of David, the son of Abraham. Abraham became the father of Isaac, Isaac of Jacob, Jacob of Judah and his brothers . . . (Matthew 1:1–2).

> This is where the good news starts—the good news of Jesus the Messiah, God's son. Isaiah the prophet put it like this ("Look! I am sending my messenger ahead of me; he will clear the way for you!"): "A shout goes up in the desert: Make way for the Lord! Clear a straight path for him!" (Mark 1:1–3).

> Many people have undertaken to draw up an orderly account of the events that have been fulfilled in our midst. It has been handed down to us by the original eyewitnesses and stewards of the word. So, most excellent Theophilus, since I had traced the course of all of it scrupulously from the start, I thought it a good idea to write an orderly account for you, so that you may have secure knowledge about the matters in which you have been instructed (Luke 1:1–4).

> In the beginning was the Word. The Word was close beside God, and the Word was God. In the beginning, he was close beside God (John 1:1–2).

When you read the introductions to the Synoptic Gospels, what similarities do you see? How is the introduction to John's Gospel different from Matthew, Mark, and Luke?

Why Were the Gospels Written?

- The first generation of disciples were dying and they wanted to capture their testimony and witness in written form.
- These stories and accounts could be used in worship.
- They were for instruction of believers in how to live for Jesus and follow the Messiah.
- They were an apologetic for the idea of a crucified and risen Messiah.

4. Read the following passages about Saul, who became Paul, recorded in the book of Acts:

> So they stoned Stephen. "Lord Jesus," he cried out, "receive my spirit." Then he knelt down and shouted at the top of his voice, "Lord, don't let this sin stand against them." Once he had said this, he fell asleep.
>
> Now Saul was giving his consent to Stephen's death.
>
> That very day a great persecution was started against the church in Jerusalem. Everyone except the apostles was scattered through the lands of Judaea and Samaria. Devout men buried Stephen, and made a great lamentation over him. But Saul was doing great damage to the church by going from one house to another, dragging off men and women and throwing them into prison (Acts 7:59–8:3).
>
> Meanwhile, Saul was still breathing out threats and murder on the Lord's disciples. He went to the high priest and requested from him official letters to the synagogues in Damascus, so that he could find people who belonged to the Way, men and women alike, tie them up, and bring them back to Jerusalem.
>
> While he was on the journey, and was getting near to Damascus, suddenly a light from heaven shone around him. He fell on the ground and heard a voice speaking to him.
>
> "Saul, Saul!" said the voice. "Why are you persecuting me?"
>
> "Who are you, Lord?" he asked.
>
> "I am Jesus," he said, "and you are persecuting me. But get up and go into the city, and it will be told you what you have to do."

The men who were traveling with Saul stood speechless. They heard the voice but couldn't see anybody. Saul got up from the ground, but when he opened his eyes he couldn't see anything. So they led him by the hand and took him to Damascus. He went for three days, being unable to see, and he neither ate nor drank (Acts 9:1–9).

"I am a Jew," he continued, "and I was born in Tarsus in Cilicia. I received my education here, in this city, and I studied at the feet of Gamaliel. I was trained in the strictest interpretations of our ancestral laws and became zealous for God, just as all of you are today. I persecuted this Way, right to the point of killing people, and I bound and handed over to prison both men and women—as the high priest and all the elders can testify. I received letters from them to the Jews of Damascus, where I was going in order to find the heretics who were there, tie them up, and bring them to Jerusalem to face their just deserts.

"Just as I was on the way, and getting near to Damascus, suddenly a bright light shone from heaven all around me. It was about midday. I fell down on the ground and I heard a voice saying, 'Saul, Saul, why are you persecuting me?' I answered, 'Who are you, Master?' And he said to me, 'I am Jesus of Nazareth, and you are persecuting me!'

"The people who were with me saw the light, but they didn't hear the voice of the person speaking to me. So I said, 'What shall I do, Master?' And the Lord said to me, 'Get up and go into Damascus, and there you will be informed of all the things that have been arranged for you to do'" (Acts 22:3–10).

How do you see Saul/Paul being transformed in these passages? How have you experienced change and transformation in your outlook, attitude, and life because of your encounter with Jesus?

5. Read the following passage from Paul's letter to the Colossians:

> Right now I'm having a celebration—a celebration of my sufferings, which are for your benefit! And I'm steadily completing, in my own flesh, what is presently lacking in the king's afflictions on behalf of his body, which is the church. I became the church's servant, according to the terms laid down by God when he gave me my commission on your behalf, the commission to fulfill God's word.
>
> This word declares the mystery that was kept secret from past ages and generations, but now has been revealed to God's holy people. God's intention was to make known to them just what rich glory this mystery contains, out there among the nations. And this is the key: the king, living within you as the hope of glory!
>
> He is the one we are proclaiming. We are instructing everybody and teaching everybody in every kind of wisdom, so that we can present everybody grown up, complete, in the king. That's what I am working for, struggling with all his energy which is powerfully at work in me (Colossians 1:24–29).

How does Paul describe his mission in this passage? How do you think this motivated him to share about Jesus and write his letters?

Paul the Theologian

Paul is a theologian of creation and new creation. He is a theologian who believes that Jesus is Israel's Messiah, that he is the Lord of the whole world, and that he is the very living embodiment of Israel's God in person. He believes God's new world has begun in Jesus through his death and resurrection. Paul is confident the resurrection of Jesus has renewed the covenant with Israel and has created a single family . . . Abraham's one family in the Messiah. This family is made up of Jews and Gentiles together.

6. Read the following brief passage from the letter of James:

> What use is it, my dear family, if someone says they have faith when they don't have works? Can faith save such a person? Supposing a brother or sister is without clothing, and is short even of daily food, and one of you says to them, "Go in peace; be warm, be full!"—but doesn't give them what their bodies need—what use is that? In the same way, faith, all by itself and without works, is dead (James 2:14–17).

In what way are works (the good things we do in the name of Jesus) a sign our faith is real? What are some of the actions and works that you know God wants you to do to show the reality and depth of your faith?

7. Read the following passage from the first letter of John:

> Love consists in this: not that we loved God, but that he loved us and sent his son to be the sacrifice that would atone for our sins. Beloved, if that's how God loved us, we ought to love one another in the same way. Nobody has ever seen God. If we love one another, God abides in us and his love is completed in us (1 John 4:10–12).

How has God revealed his love to lost and sinful people? How does his love inspire and teach you how to show love to others?

8. Read the following passage from the book of Revelation:

> Then I saw a new heaven and a new earth. The first heaven and the first earth had passed away, and there was no longer any sea. And I saw the holy city, the new Jerusalem, coming down out of heaven, from God, prepared like a bride dressed up for her husband. I heard a loud voice from the throne, and this is what it said: "Look! God has come to dwell with humans! He will dwell with them, and they will be his people, and God himself will be with them and will be their God. He will wipe away every tear from their eyes. There will be no more death or mourning or weeping or pain anymore, since the first things have passed away."

The one who sat on the throne said, "Look, I am making all things new." And he said, "Write, because these words are faithful and true."

Then he said to me, "It is done! I am the Alpha and the Omega, the beginning and the end. I will freely give water to the thirsty, water from the spring of the water of life. The one who conquers will inherit these things. I will be his God and he shall be my son (Revelation 21:1–7).

What kind of things happen when heaven meets earth? How do you see God doing these kinds of things in the person and power of Jesus today?

All Things New

Many Christian teachers imagine that the purpose of Christian discipleship is one day we will leave this earth and go up to heaven. Instead, the end of the book of Revelation is about the heavenly city, the new Jerusalem, coming down to earth so that the dwelling of God is with humans and God says, "I am making everything new."

CLOSING PRAYER

Take time as a group to pray in some of the following directions . . .

- Thank God for the people who have taught you the truth and lessons of the Bible. Mention them by name and express to God your deep appreciation for placing these people in your life.
- Ask the Holy Spirit to give you many eye-opening moments over these eight sessions where you see the New Testament in a new light and with fresh insight.
- Lift up praise to Jesus for bringing heaven to earth (including to your life).
- Ask God to make your mind sharp so that you can understand how he has brought together the twenty-seven books of the New Testament into one message of God's work through the Messiah, Jesus.
- Pray for eyes to see where God is still bringing heaven to earth and ask for power to share in this work of Jesus that continues in our day.

Between-Sessions Personal Study

Reflect on the content you've covered this week in *The New Testament You Never Knew* by engaging in any or all of the following between-sessions activities. The time you invest will be well spent, so let God use it to draw you closer to him. At your next meeting, share with your group any key points or insights that stood out to you as you spent this time with the Lord.

REFLECTION

Why do you think God used so many different people to write the story of the Messiah in the New Testament?

Why do you think God chose Saul, a persecutor of the church, to become a primary leader in the early church, a preacher of Jesus, and the writer of so many New Testament books?

What specific actions can you take during the next eight weeks to become more familiar with the New Testament and the story of Jesus that it tells?

Write down a prayer asking God to guide you to the insights and truths that he wants you to learn as you go through this study.

STUDY

Commit to spending some time during the upcoming week (until your group meets again) to read the following portions of the New Testament each day. Write down one new lesson and new insight you learned about Jesus from your daily reading.

Day 1: The Gospels

Read Luke 1–2; Matthew 5–6; Mark 15–16; and John 1–2

One new lesson you learned . . .

One insight you gained about Jesus . . .

Day 2: The Book of Acts
Read Acts 1–2; 9; 16; and 25

One new lesson you learned . . .

One insight you gained about Jesus . . .

Day 3: The Letters of Paul
Read Romans 3; Galatians 1; Ephesians 2; Philippians 2; and Colossians 1

One new lesson you learned . . .

One insight you gained about Jesus . . .

Day 4: The General Letters
Read Hebrews 1–3; James 1–2; 1 Peter 1; 1 John 1; and Jude

One new lesson you learned . . .

One insight you gained about Jesus . . .

Day 5: The Book of Revelation
Read Revelation 1–4; 19; and 21–22

One new lesson you learned . . .

One insight you gained about Jesus . . .

RESPONSE

Read through the insights you recorded about Jesus this past week. In the space below, write down three key insights and how they should (1) impact the way you relate to Jesus, and (2) impact the way you relate to the people in your life.

Insight #1

What you learned about Jesus . . .

How this should influence your faith and relationship with God . . .

How this should impact your relationship with the people God has placed in your life . . .

Insight #2

What you learned about Jesus . . .

How this should influence your faith and relationship with God . . .

How this should impact your relationship with the people God has placed in your life . . .

Insight #3

What you learned about Jesus . . .

How this should influence your faith and relationship with God . . .

How this should impact your relationship with the people God has placed in your life . . .

APPLICATION

The followers of Jesus believed a new world had begun in Christ through his death and resurrection. God had dealt with sin and evil, and his covenant with Israel now consisted of a single family—a family comprised of Jews and Gentiles together. This understanding of Jesus affected their personal lives, their relationships, and the way they viewed the world around them. Think about how your understanding of Jesus has impacted you in each of these same three ways and record your responses below.

In your personal life . . .

In your relationships . . .

In the world around you—your church, culture, and community . . .

FOR NEXT WEEK

Use the space below to write any key insights or questions from your personal study that you want to discuss at the next group meeting.

THE WORLD OF JESUS AND THE APOSTLES

When the first Christians began to spread throughout
the world, they faced some important questions:
How could they be in the world but not of the world?
How much of Greek culture could they absorb?
They were facing many of the same questions
as the Jewish people of the day. How do
they live in the city and yet be faithful
to their own God and way of life?
MICHAEL F. BIRD

INTRODUCTION

In his bestselling book *Outliers: The Story of Success*, Malcolm Gladwell digs deeply into the reasons some people succeed and others do not. As in all of his books, Gladwell takes the reader through a series of twists and turns that lead to surprising and unexpected insights.

One of the conclusions Gladwell reaches in the book is that, for many people, being born in the *right place* makes all the difference. In addition, the *timing* of a person's arrival on planet earth has a huge impact on the potential for him or her to succeed. Gladwell shows that regardless of the type of success—whether it's the victories of athletes, or the mind-blowing popularity of the Beatles, or Bill Gates's efforts in helping launch the modern digital age—timing and location are always significant factors in success.

The problem is that none of us has any choice as to when or where we will be born. From a human perspective, it is absolutely random . . . a genetic and historical roll of the proverbial dice. Only God has the power to decide who will be born, when they will be born, and where they will arrive on the world map. As King David once wrote, "Your eyes beheld my unformed substance. In your book were written all the days that were formed for me, when none of them as yet existed" (Psalm 139:16).

The only person in all history who had input as to where and when he would be born was Jesus. As the second person of the Trinity and fully divine, Jesus knew the perfect time and ideal location in which to be born. His mission would be to make disciples of all nations—from Jerusalem to the ends of the earth. Success would be measured by how quickly that message spread and how people responded to the life-changing story of this man who claimed to be God, was rejected, abused, and crucified . . . then rose from the grave and ascended into heaven.

If it had been up to a human strategist to plan the successful entry of God into history, it is unlikely he or she would have chosen locations like Bethlehem, Nazareth, and Galilee. It would be far-fetched to believe such a strategist would choose a time in history with so much radical political upheaval and transition of national powers. And certainly no one with any sense would have chosen the parents of this heavenly king—a poor carpenter (or possibly stone mason) and a young Jewish virgin girl. None of it made sense . . . from a human standpoint.

Thankfully, God did not ask our opinion! Drawing on his own divine wisdom, he entered our world in obscurity and with humility. He chose the perfect time and the ideal place . . and the rest, as they say, is history.

TALK ABOUT IT

If you or any of your group members are just meeting for the first time, take a few minutes to introduce yourselves and share any insights you have from last week's personal study. Then, to get things started, discuss one of the following questions:

- What is a success or accomplishment you have experienced that was influenced, in some part, by where you were born, whom you were born to, and when you were born?

—or—

- If you have some understanding of the cultural, economic, political, and religious environment of the world into which Jesus was born, how was this just the right time for heaven to intersect with earth in the coming of Jesus?

Key Dates

322 BC Alexander the Great conquers the ancient near east and Judea.

167 BC Antiochus Epiphanes desecrates the temple in Jerusalem.

160 BC The end of the Maccabean wars leads to a century of Jewish rule in Judea.

63 BC Pompey enters Jerusalem.

27 BC Octavian becomes the sole ruler of the Roman Empire (including Judea).

VIDEO TEACHING NOTES

Play the video segment for session two. As you watch the video, use the space provided to collect thoughts and notes about the New Testament that are fresh and new for you.

The Jewish World

The significance of the synagogue

Roman taxation and political systems

The Pharisees, Sadducees, and Essenes

Jewish Hopes

As the Jewish people of Jesus' day looked back and thought about who they were, they wanted God to do something that would enable their culture to flourish. They wanted God to cleanse their religion, their temple, once and for all so his people would finally get it together.

The Greek World

Spread of the Greek people and culture

Spread of Greek philosophy and religion

Challenges Christians faced living in a Greek culture

The Gymnasium

An ancient gymnasium wasn't just a place for athletic competition and conditioning of the body. It was a place where men could train both their body and their mind. It was also a place for them to gather and meet with their peers to cultivate social networks.

The Roman World

Rome's control of the Mediterranean world

Julius Caesar and Octavian (Augustus)

The symbols of Rome and what they communicated

Challenges Christians faced living under Roman rule

What's in a Name?

The followers of Jesus, the Messiah, were known by several names during the early centuries of the church, including "the Nazarenes" (see Matthew 2:23), "Followers of the Way" (see Acts 9:2, 9, 23), and "Christians" (see Acts 11:26; 26:28; 1 Peter 4:16).

GROUP DISCUSSION

Take a few minutes to discuss what you just watched and explore these concepts together.

1. The Jewish people were familiar with the invasions of their land by the Greeks, the Syrians, and the Romans and were longing for a *lasting* kingdom that reflected their beliefs and convictions. What were some of the cultural, religious, and political realities the Jewish people were facing that most troubled them?

2. How had these centuries of invasion, occupation, and oppression created a deep longing in the Jewish people for the kingdom of God? How did this create an environment that was ideal for the coming of Jesus and his rule and reign?

3. Read the following scene, which occurred in the synagogue of Capernaum:

> Jesus went down to Capernaum, a town of Galilee. He used to teach them every sabbath. They were astonished at his teaching, because his message was powerful and authoritative.
>
> There was a man in the synagogue who had the spirit of an unclean demon.
>
> "Hey, you!" he yelled out at the top of his voice. "What's going on with you and me, Jesus of Nazareth? Have you come to destroy us? I know who you are—you're God's Holy One!"
>
> "Shut up!" Jesus rebuked him. "Come out of him!"
>
> The demon threw the man down right there in front of them, and came out without harming him. Fear came over them all. "What's all this?" they started to say to one another. "He's got power! He's got authority! He tells the unclean spirits what to do, and they come out!" Word about him went out to the whole surrounding region (Luke 4:31–37).

If you had been in the synagogue in Capernaum on that day and you were hungry for a Jewish Messiah to arise and set your nation free, how would an encounter like this have impacted you and the others who were gathered there?

The Jewish Synagogue

The Greek word "synagogue" means a place where the community would come together. It was far more than just a place of worship—it was also a hub of economic business, social interaction, political action, and cultural engagement.

4. Read the following prophetic passages, which during Jesus' day were familiar and read in worship in local synagogues:

> Get you up to a high mountain,
>   O Zion, herald of good tidings;
> lift up your voice with strength,
>   O Jerusalem, herald of good tidings,
>   lift it up, do not fear;
> say to the cities of Judah,
>   "Here is your God!"
>   See, the Lord God comes with might,
>   and his arm rules for him;
> his reward is with him,
>   and his recompense before him.
> He will feed his flock like a shepherd;
>   he will gather the lambs in his arms,
> and carry them in his bosom,
>   and gently lead the mother sheep (Isaiah 40:9–11).

And in the days of those kings the God of heaven will set up a kingdom that shall never be destroyed, nor shall this kingdom be left to another people. It shall crush all these kingdoms and bring them to an end, and it shall stand forever; just as you saw that a stone was cut from the mountain not by hands, and that it crushed the iron, the bronze, the clay, the silver, and the gold. The great God has informed the king what shall be hereafter. The dream is certain, and its interpretation trustworthy (Daniel 2:44–45).

As I watched in the night visions,

> I saw one like a human being
>> coming with the clouds of heaven.
> And he came to the Ancient One
>> and was presented before him.
> To him was given dominion
>> and glory and kingship,
> that all peoples, nations, and languages
>> should serve him.
> His dominion is an everlasting dominion
>> that shall not pass away,
> and his kingship is one
>> that shall never be destroyed (Daniel 7:13–14).

How did these passages point to the coming Messiah and the kingdom he would bring? How do you think these passages would have been understood by the people of Jesus' day?

5. In the first century, Christians grappled with the question of how to participate in culture without compromising their faith. Why is this still an important question for us to answer today? How would *you* answer this question?

6. The Roman Emperor Octavian declared that he had brought peace and salvation to the world and was the source of justice. He was declared the "divine son of god." How were Octavian's and Jesus' claims similar? How were they radically different?

The Rise of Augustus

On August 1 in 30 BC, Gaius Octavius Thurinus, better known to us as "Augustus," crushed the combined forces of his former co-leader, Marcus Antony, and Cleopatra of Egypt at the Battle of Actium. The decisive victory left Augustus as the sole master of the Roman Empire.

7. In light of what you have learned during this session, how has your understanding of the conflict surrounding Jesus' ministry deepened? What are some things you have read in the New Testament that make more sense now?

8. The leaders of Jesus' day saw Christianity as a subversive philosophy and way of life. These Jesus-following people had their own ruler (or Lord), were committed to changing the culture, and would only follow Jesus . . . while still being good citizens. How do you think the leaders in Jesus' day would have responded to these kinds of people?

CLOSING PRAYER

Take time as a group to pray in some of the following directions . . .

- Thank the Father for the beauty of his timing and placement of Jesus into history exactly when and where he did.
- Thank God for when and where he placed you when you were born. Acknowledge he is wiser than you and commit to embrace where he has placed you.
- Ask God to give you strength to live for Jesus no matter how difficult the situation in the world might become.
- Pray for you and for your group members to show the love of Jesus and speak the message of Jesus even when it is challenging.
- Pray for your local church to be a place where believers could gather, worship, share life, encourage each other, and create a place for genuine spiritual growth that leads to cultural transformation.

Between-Sessions Personal Study

Reflect on the content you've covered this week in *The New Testament You Never Knew* by engaging in any or all of the following between-sessions activities. The time you invest will be well spent, so let God use it to draw you closer to him. At your next meeting, share with your group any key points or insights that stood out to you as you spent this time with the Lord.

REFLECTION

How did the Old Testament prophets prepare the way for the coming of the Messiah?

How was the world ripe for the coming of Jesus, the promised Messiah?

How did God prepare you to encounter Jesus and invite him to be the ruler of your life?

Write down a prayer of thanks to God for being sovereign over all history and over your life.

STUDY

Commit to spending some time this week to read the following portions of the New Testament and reflect on what you learn about the people who are mentioned. Also keep in mind what you have learned about both the political and religious leaders in the New Testament world.

Day 1: Matthew 16

Your insights about the people mentioned in this account . . .

Day 2: John 18

Your insights about the people mentioned in this account . . .

Day 3: Acts 19

Your insights about the people mentioned in this account . . .

Day 4: Acts 22

Your insights about the people mentioned in this account . . .

Day 5: Acts 23–24

Your insights about the people mentioned in this account . . .

RESPONSE

Do an online study this week of the following characters or groups. Write down two to three things you learn about each that help you to better understand the New Testament story.

Alexander the Great

Antiochus Epiphanes

Pompey

Octavian (Augustus)

The Pharisees

The Sadducees

APPLICATION

As our world and culture continue to change, it is important for parents and grandparents to pray for the next generation and model what it looks like to be in the world but not of it. Jesus' early followers did not want to blend in with culture—they wanted to be a light on a hill shining the very presence of the Messiah. The early followers wanted to see the kingdom of God break into the world and hungered to create a new culture that honored God and lifted up Jesus.

Pray for the Next Generation

With this in mind, write down three ways you can pray for the next generation (your own family members, young people in your church, and the next generation in the world around you). Take time to pray each of these prayers daily during the coming week.

Teach the Next Generation

Write down three lessons you have learned about how to follow Jesus even when the current of the world is flowing in the opposite direction. Think about how you have lived in counter-cultural ways, what makes it difficult to do so, and why it has been worth it for you personally. Consider how you can share these lessons with one or two people you know this week.

FOR NEXT WEEK

Use the space below to write any key insights or questions from your personal study that you want to discuss at the next group meeting.

THE LIFE AND DEATH OF JESUS

When we see Jesus announcing the kingdom of God, we also see him doing all kinds of things like healing people and celebrating with all the wrong kind of folk—and then explaining this is what it looks like when God becomes King. It is not what people expected.

N.T. WRIGHT

INTRODUCTION

If you did a Google search on the name "Jesus," you would find around 827,000,000 results. If you began reading those results, you would discover a vast array of responses to the question, *who is Jesus?*

Many call him a great moral teacher.

Others frame him as a prophet or a religious leader.

Some claim that Jesus is fully God, fully divine, and fully human . . . mysteriously, all at the same time.

Some paint a picture of a man who was a revolutionary.

Others describe him as an advocate for the poor—a man of compassion who cared about the forgotten, the marginalized, and the outcast.

Many people see Jesus as a great healer and miracle worker.

Lots of people see him as a friend and a personal companion.

Entire groups of people embrace Jesus as the Lord (leader) of their lives.

What is amazing is that all of these responses to the question about Jesus' identity embrace a part of who he actually was. These responses all shed light on the remarkable story of the Messiah and Savior who chose to leave heaven and walk among the people.

Yet along with these descriptions is one that often does not get the attention it deserves: *Jesus was the bringer of a new kingdom.* He came introducing the reality that the kingdom of God was present and breaking into history. He then made it crystal clear he was the King who would rule the kingdom. With astounding grace, Jesus invited ordinary people to enter the kingdom life he came to offer to all who were willing to accept it.

As the story of Jesus unfolds, we are swept into the reality that Jesus did not come into this world just to reform, change, or tweak the existing world systems and power structures. Rather, he came as the King of all kings and the ruler of a new order: the kingdom of God.

TALK ABOUT IT

Welcome to the third session of *The New Testament You Never Knew.* To get things started, discuss one of the following questions as a group:

- Think about how you pictured Jesus in your mind when you were young. How would you have answered the question, *Who is Jesus?* What shaped the picture or idea you had of Jesus when you were a child?

—*or*—

- When you think of Jesus being the King over all kings and the one who came to bring his kingdom into this world, what do you imagine Jesus wants his kingdom to look like?

God's Kingdom Agenda

When Jesus says, "Blessings on the poor in spirit . . . blessings on the meek . . . blessings on people who hunger and thirst for God's justice . . . blessings on the peacemakers" (Matthew 5:3, 5–6, 9) he is not just saying this is the type of character that God will bless. Rather, Jesus is saying this is God's kingdom agenda and this is the kingdom vocation. This is the means through which God will bless the world.

VIDEO TEACHING NOTES

Play the video segment for session three. As you watch, use the space provided to collect your thoughts and make some notes about the New Testament that are new and fresh for you.

Jesus' Ministry Begins

Jesus' early life in Nazareth and Sepphoris

The significance of Jesus' baptism and temptation in the wilderness

Jesus' Kingdom Message

Jesus' use of stories to explain how the kingdom of God is not as people imagined

Jesus issues a fresh version of Israel's vocation (the Sermon on the Mount)

How God Changes the World

In Jesus' day, people assumed that if God was going to do something to rid the world of evil, he would "send in the tanks" and just blast everything out of the way. But Jesus explains this is not the way in which God works. Jesus says that when God wants to change the world, he sends in the meek, the mourners, the brokenhearted, and those who are hungry for justice. These are the people he uses to transform the world.

Jesus' View of the Messiah

Jesus redefines the messianic role to his disciples at Caesarea Philippi

Jesus emphasizes his mission . . . sacrifice and the cross

Passion Week

Jesus rides on a donkey into Jerusalem (parodying a Roman kingly procession) and cleanses the temple (an acted parable)

Jesus explains to his disciples what his death was going to be about (Passover meal)

The Crucifixion

How the Gospel writers described what Jesus' death meant

Historical and theological reasons why Jesus had to die—and why both reasons actually go together

Crucifixion

Crucifixion was a horrible and brutal way of killing a person—and the Romans knew it. They not only used crucifixion as a method of executing people but also as a means of propaganda. Crucifixion expressed the zenith of degradation, death, and disempowerment. It was the worst possible punishment the Romans reserved for the worst possible people.

GROUP DISCUSSION

Take a few minutes to discuss what you just watched and explore these concepts together.

1. What is one story from the life of Jesus that sticks out in your mind? What in particular about this story moves you?

2. Read the following passage describing John the Baptist's wilderness ministry:

> John himself had clothing made from camel's hair, and a leather belt around his waist. His food was locusts and wild honey. Jerusalem, and all Judaea, and the whole area around the Jordan, were going off to him. They were being baptized by him in the river Jordan, confessing their sins.
>
> He saw several Pharisees and Sadducees coming to be baptized by him.
>
> "You brood of vipers!" he said to them. "Who warned you to escape from the coming wrath? You'd better prove your repentance by bearing the right sort of fruit! And you needn't start thinking to yourselves, 'We have Abraham as our father.' Let me tell you, God is quite capable of raising up children for Abraham from these stones! The axe is already taking aim at

the root of the tree. Every tree that doesn't produce good fruit is to be cut down and thrown into the fire.

"I am baptizing you with water, for repentance," John continued. "But the one who is coming behind me is more powerful than me! I'm not even worthy to carry his sandals. He will baptize you with the holy spirit and fire! He's got his shovel in his hand, ready to clear out his barn, and gather all his corn into the granary. But he'll burn up the chaff with a fire that will never go out" (Matthew 3:4–12).

John did *not* call the people to passively wait for the Messiah. What significant changes did he call the people to make in anticipation of Jesus' coming? How was his baptizing ministry a kind of new exodus for the people?

Baptism in the Jordan River

John baptized people to prepare them for the "new exodus" that was about to come. It is believed John chose to baptize in the Jordan River because centuries earlier the Israelites had crossed into the Promised Land through it. John was saying, in effect, that this was about to happen again. God was going to bring about a new exodus . . . and the people needed to get ready for it.

3. The people in Jesus' day were expecting the Messiah to be a military leader who would set them free and set up a new kingdom. Even John the Baptist seemed to have this picture of the Messiah in his mind. But how was Jesus' vision of the coming kingdom and his role quite different than what most of the people were expecting?

4. Read the following story about Jesus' temptation in the wilderness:

> Jesus returned from the Jordan, filled with the spirit. The spirit took him off into the wilderness for forty days, to be tested by the devil. He ate nothing during that time, and at the end of it he was hungry.
>
> "If you are God's son," said the devil, "tell this stone to become a loaf of bread."
>
> "It is written," replied Jesus, "'It takes more than bread to keep you alive.'"
>
> The devil then took him up and showed him, in an instant, all the kingdoms of the world.
>
> "I will give you authority over all of this," said the devil, "and all the prestige that goes with it. It's been given to me, you see, and I give it to anyone I like. So it can all be yours . . . if you will just worship me."
>
> "It is written," replied Jesus, "'The Lord your God is the one you must worship; he is the only one you must serve.'"
>
> Then the devil took him to Jerusalem and stood him on a pinnacle of the Temple.
>
> "If you are God's son," he said, "throw yourself down from here; it's written, 'He will give his angels a command about you, to look after you'; and 'They will carry you in their hands, so that you won't hit your foot against a stone.'"
>
> "It has been said," replied Jesus, "'You mustn't put the Lord your God to the test.'"
>
> When the devil had finished each temptation, he left him until another opportunity (Luke 4:1–13).

There is a stark contrast between Israel's failure during their time of temptation in the wilderness and Jesus' victory over the tempter. How does Jesus prove to be faithful to God during his time of temptation? How did this victory over the enemy launch Jesus into the public phase of his kingdom ministry?

5. Read the following account of Jesus' teaching to his disciples in Caesarea Philippi:

> Jesus came to Caesarea Philippi. There he put this question to his disciples: "Who do people say that the son of man is?"
>
> "John the Baptist," they replied. "Others say Elijah. Others say Jeremiah, or one of the prophets."
>
> "What about you?" he asked them. "Who do you say I am?"
>
> Simon Peter answered, "You're the Messiah. You're the son of the living God!"
>
> "God's blessing on you, Simon, son of John!" answered Jesus. "Flesh and blood didn't reveal that to you; it was my father in heaven. And I've got something to tell you, too: you are Peter, the rock, and on this rock I will build my church, and the gates of hell won't overpower it. I will give you the keys of the kingdom of heaven. Whatever you tie up on earth will have been tied up in heaven, and whatever you untie on earth will have been untied in heaven."
>
> Then he sternly ordered the disciples not to tell anyone that he was the Messiah (Matthew 16:13–20).

How did Jesus redefine the messianic role in the minds of his followers? How did Jesus prepare them for his upcoming passion and crucifixion?

6. Read the following passage describing Jesus' actions in the temple:

> Jesus went into the Temple and threw out all the people who were buying and selling in the Temple. He upturned the tables of the money-changers and the seats of the dove-sellers.
>
> "This is what the Bible says," he said to them,
>
> "'My house will be called a house of prayer—But you have made it a brigands' lair!'"
>
> The blind and the lame came to him in the Temple, and he healed them. But when the chief priests and the scribes saw the remarkable things he was doing, and the children shouting out "Hosanna to David's son!" in the Temple, they were very cross.
>
> "Do you hear what they're saying?" they asked Jesus. "Yes," said Jesus. "Did you never read what it says,
>
> 'You called forth praise to rise to you from newborn babes and infants too!'" (Matthew 21:12–16).

What did this public act of Jesus declare about who he was? Why were his actions in the temple so explosive and inflammatory?

Who Has Authority Over the Temple?

Jesus' act of "cleansing" the temple implied to the people that he had authority over it. King David had planned the temple, King Solomon had built it, and King Hezekiah had cleansed it. These were all kings of Israel—the temple and royalty went hand in hand. So when Jesus cleared out the temple, he was clearly doing something that implied he had that same kind of authority!

7. Read the following prophecy from Zechariah and the account of Jesus entering Jerusalem:

> Rejoice greatly, Daughter Zion!
>   Shout, Daughter Jerusalem!
> See, your king comes to you,
>   righteous and victorious,
> lowly and riding on a donkey,
>   on a colt, the foal of a donkey.
> I will take away the chariots from Ephraim
>   and the warhorses from Jerusalem,
> and the battle bow will be broken.
>   He will proclaim peace to the nations.
> His rule will extend from sea to sea
>   and from the River to the ends of the earth
>   (Zechariah 9:9–10).

They brought it to Jesus, threw their cloaks on the colt, and mounted Jesus on it. As he was going along, people kept spreading their cloaks on the road.

When he came to the descent of the Mount of Olives, the whole crowd of disciples began to celebrate and praise God at the tops of their voices for all the powerful deeds they had seen.

"Welcome, welcome, welcome with a blessing," they sang.

"Welcome to the king in the name of the Lord! Peace in heaven, and glory on high!"

Some of the Pharisees from the crowd said to Jesus, "Teacher, tell your disciples to stop that."

"Let me tell you," replied Jesus, "if they stayed silent, the stones would be shouting out!" (Luke 19:35–40).

How did Jesus embrace the vision of a humble servant and reject the expectation of a coming conquering king? What are some practical ways you can emulate the humility of your King?

8. What are some of the historical reasons that Jesus died on the cross? What are some of the theological reasons Jesus had to suffer a shameful death on the cross?

Kingdom and Cross

The Gospel writers tell about Jesus' achievement at the cross in terms of God doing something in his kingdom that breaks the power of evil once and for all. The cross is all about how the kingdom work of Jesus is completed. It doesn't make sense to say that God is now becoming king unless we understand how the radical power of evil was defeated at the cross.

CLOSING PRAYER

Take time as a group to pray in some of the following directions . . .

- Thank Jesus that he came as a humble servant and not as a political conqueror.
- Ask God to help you grow as a humble servant and not as one who has to always win every human conflict.
- Pray for the kingdom of God to break fully into our world . . . starting in your own heart and home.
- Ask God to give you the power of the Holy Spirit to resist the temptations the enemy brings your way.
- Pray for the absolute kingship of Jesus to rule over your life so you will yield to him in all things at all times.

Between-Sessions Personal Study

Reflect on the content you've covered this week in *The New Testament You Never Knew* by engaging in any or all of the following between-sessions activities. The time you invest will be well spent, so let God use it to draw you closer to him. At your next meeting, share with your group any key points or insights that stood out to you as you spent this time with the Lord.

REFLECTION

How did Jesus show up in ways that surprised and shocked the people of his day and how has he showed up in your life in amazing and surprising ways?

Spend some more time praying and reflecting on ways you need the kingdom to break into your heart, life, home, church, community, and world?

What are ways that Jesus suffered and sacrificed for us through his incarnation, life, and death? How is he calling you to sacrifice for him?

Write a prayer surrendering areas of your life that you are still holding on to and not surrendering to Jesus, the Messiah. Tell him that you are willing to follow and let go of whatever he wants you to give to him.

STUDY

Commit to spending some time this week to read the following chapters from the Gospel of Luke. Write down (1) what you learn about Jesus, the Messiah, and (2) what you learn about the kingdom that Jesus brought to our world and our lives.

Day 1: Luke 4–6

What you learned about Jesus . . .

What you learned about the kingdom Jesus brought . . .

Day 2: Luke 7–9

What you learned about Jesus . . .

What you learned about the kingdom Jesus brought . . .

Day 3: Luke 10–12

What you learned about Jesus . . .

What you learned about the kingdom Jesus brought . . .

Day 4: Luke 16–18

What you learned about Jesus . . .

What you learned about the kingdom Jesus brought . . .

Day 5: Luke 19–21

What you learned about Jesus . . .

What you learned about the kingdom Jesus brought . . .

RESPONSE

Identify two areas of temptation you battle against in your life. Write these in the space below (or, if you feel this is too private, just think about these as you do this exercise in your heart and mind). Once you have identified the temptations, select one of the passages below that you feel will help you battle against that specific temptation. Commit these passages to memory and speak them out (verbally or in your heart) each time you feel tempted this week.

Area of Temptation #1:

Area of Temptation #2:

Scripture Memory Passages

Trust in the LORD with all your heart, and do not rely on your own insight. In all your ways acknowledge him, and he will make straight your paths (Proverbs 3:5–6).

For he will deliver you from the snare of the fowler and from the deadly pestilence; he will cover you with his pinions, and under his wings you will find refuge; his faithfulness is a shield and buckler (Psalm 91:3–4).

I treasure your word in my heart, so that I may not sin against you (Psalm 119:11).

Run away from immorality. Every sin that it's possible for someone to commit happens outside the body; but immorality involves sinning against your own body (1 Corinthians 6:18).

Every test that comes upon you is normal for human beings. But God is faithful: he won't let you be tested beyond your ability. Along with the testing, he will provide the way of escape, so that you can bear it (1 Corinthians 10:13).

Live by the spirit, and you won't do what the flesh wants you to do (Galatians 5:16).

Be strong in the Lord, and in the strength of his power. Put on God's complete armor. Then you'll be able to stand firm against the devil's trickery (Ephesians 6:10–11).

I have strength for everything in the one who gives me power (Philippians 4:13).

God's blessing on the man who endures testing! When he has passed the test, he will receive the crown of life, which God has promised to those who love him (James 1:12).

Resist [the devil], staying resolute in your faith, and knowing that other family members in the rest of the world are facing identical sufferings (1 Peter 5:9).

APPLICATION

For followers of Jesus, the kingdom of God and the cross are always bound together. Read the passion narrative in each of the four Gospels listed below and write down how you see the kingdom of God linked to the cross of Jesus.

Matthew 26–28

Mark 14–15

Luke 22–24

John 19–21

FOR NEXT WEEK

Use the space below to write any key insights or questions from your personal study that you want to discuss at the next group meeting.

THE RESURRECTION OF JESUS

The early church was driven by the belief that Jesus had been raised from the dead. It wasn't just an ancillary belief or an accessory. The early believers saw themselves as part of a resurrection movement, and their preaching, prayers, hopes, dreams of the future, symbols, and what they did and said were all permeated by this belief that Jesus was risen.

MICHAEL F. BIRD

INTRODUCTION

If we were able to see our lives as a timeline, we could identify exact days, hours, and even seconds when everything changes. These are moments that mark the beginning of a whole new season. Sometimes they are delightful beyond expression . . . while at other times, they lead to a period of struggle and a time of stormy uncertainty.

A couple stands at the altar. They are wearing the finest of clothes and are surrounded on this day by their family and friends. Vows are given and rings are exchanged. A pastor then speaks the words, "I now pronounce you husband and wife!" In a sense, the man and woman are the same people as they were before these words were spoken. However, in a very real way, everything else has changed. Their lives will never be the same.

A doctor sits across from an anxious woman. She has been through a long series of tests and procedures conducted by a number of specialists. The doctor's face is somber and serious. The words come with mind-numbing force: "I am sorry to tell you that the tests show cancer in both your lungs." With one sentence—just fifteen words—her whole life has changed.

A man comes home from work. At dinner, his wife seems unusually happy and bubbly. There is a twinkle in her eyes and an excitement in the tone of her words. When the man asks what is going on, the wife responds, "I was going to wait to tell you until after dinner, but I can't hold it in any longer . . . we're going to have a baby!"

In the history of the world, there is one specific moment that stands out among the rest—a moment that unleashed amazing power, joy, and hope. It marked the beginning of an entirely new understanding of life and eternity. This moment draws a line in heaven, earth, and human hearts. Three words mark the start of this era, which continues today and will last forever: *"He is risen!"*

The resurrection of Jesus surprised everyone in the ancient world. Even those who held a belief in some kind of afterlife did not imagine that a person could come back from the grave after being crucified and buried. No one saw it coming.

The moment Jesus rose from the dead, everything changed. And because he rose and is alive today, everything continues to change!

TALK ABOUT IT

Welcome to the fourth session of *The New Testament You Never Knew*. To get things started, discuss one of the following questions as a group:

- Think about a moment in your life when everything suddenly changed. What happened? How did things change . . . for better or for worse?

—*or*—

- When you think about the resurrection of Jesus, what does this event and moment in history mean for your life today?

Various Views of Resurrection
In the ancient world, resurrection meant different things to different people. If you were to ask a leader in a synagogue in Athens, he would have explained resurrection one way. If you went up the road to the Areopagus and talked to the people there, they would have said resurrection meant something else. The two groups would have thought of entirely different things.

VIDEO TEACHING NOTES

Play the video segment for session four. As you watch, use the space provided to collect your thoughts and make some notes about the New Testament that are new and fresh for you.

Greco-Roman View of the Afterlife
The Greek view of coming back from death—revolting, abhorrent, and revolutionary

A message that is counterintuitive to the Greco-Roman world

Greco-Roman Views of Resurrection

An ancient Greek author wrote that when a man has died and the dust has soaked up his blood, there is no resurrection. Similarly, the Roman poet Horace said about a friend who had died that he was in a sleep from which men never recover. For the Greeks, there was no resurrection.

Jewish Views of the Afterlife

The Jewish view of God—creator of the world and ruler over life and death

A shift in Jewish thinking during the second century BC

Revolutionary Thinking

If we look at the revolutionary movements around the time of Jesus, what we see are people who were consumed with the belief that God was going to do a new thing. God was going to raise the dead and vindicate his people. Therefore, what they had to do in the present was be loyal to him so that even if they died seeking to accomplish his will, he would raise them to new life. It was this kind of hope that surrounded and inspired so many of the early Christians.

The Sadducees' and Pharisees' perspective on resurrection

What resurrection affirmed in the Jewish way of thinking

How the early church reread the Old Testament in light of Jesus' resurrection

Rereading the Old Testament Texts

The early Christians, in light of what they believed about Jesus' resurrection, started to reread the ancient biblical texts with new eyes and ears. They read and understood them in ways they hadn't read them before. They knew God would one day raise his people from the dead, but they started to see their resurrection through the resurrection of Jesus. With this in mind, they read the Old Testament passages about resurrection through the lens of the empty tomb.

Evidence for the Resurrection

The evidence of the empty tomb and first witnesses

The evidence of the resurrection appearances

The evidence of the beliefs of the early church . . . and implications of that belief

What the Resurrection Affirms

Belief in the resurrection is a way of affirming two key concepts. First, it affirms that our God is the creator of the world and that he is going to re-create this world. Second, it affirms that our God is a God of justice who will ultimately put all things right.

GROUP DISCUSSION

Take a few minutes to discuss what you just watched and explore these concepts together.

1. In light of what you learned in the teaching, how was the Jewish understanding of the resurrection different than the Greco-Roman understanding of the afterlife? How would Jesus' resurrection have been a surprise to those who embraced either viewpoint?

2. Read the following passage about the importance of the resurrection:

> Let me remind you, brothers and sisters, about the good news which I announced to you. You received this good news, and you're standing firm on it, and you are saved through it, if you hold fast the message I announced to you—unless it was for nothing that you believed!
>
> What I handed on to you at the beginning, you see, was what I received, namely this: "The Messiah died for our sins in accordance with the Bible; he was buried; he was raised on the third day in accordance with the Bible; he was seen by Cephas, then by the Twelve; then he was seen by over five hundred brothers and sisters at once, most of whom are still with us, though some fell asleep; then he was seen by James, then by all the apostles; and, last of all, as to one ripped from the womb, he appeared even to me" (1 Corinthians 15:1–8).

The early Christians knew both the Jewish and Roman world did not embrace their understanding of resurrection. What obstacles did the early church have to overcome in order to help people embrace Jesus as the risen Messiah?

3. Read the following passage from the book of Daniel in the Old Testament:

> At that time Michael, the great prince, the protector of your people, shall arise. There shall be a time of anguish, such as has never occurred since nations first came into existence. But at that time your people shall be delivered, everyone who is found written in the book. Many of those who sleep in the dust of the earth shall awake, some to everlasting life, and some to shame and everlasting contempt. Those who are wise shall shine like the brightness of the sky, and those who lead many to righteousness, like the stars forever and ever (Daniel 12:1–3).

How would a passage like this have affirmed the new understanding of resurrection that Jesus brought through his life, teaching, and resurrection?

Weighing the Evidence

Is there any evidence of Jesus' resurrection? Obviously, we can't prove that it happened with any kind of certainty. But If we weigh up all the evidence—if we look at all the factors and all the witnesses to the event—the logic of history is that Jesus indeed rose from the dead.

4. How does the reality of the empty tomb strengthen your faith today? If Jesus had not risen from the dead and the tomb was not empty, how would this change the Christian faith and your life?

5. Read the following accounts of the post-resurrection appearances of Jesus:

> On the evening of that day, the first day of the week, the doors were shut where the disciples were, for fear of the Judaeans. Jesus came and stood in the middle of them.
>
> "Peace be with you," he said.
>
> With these words, he showed them his hands and his side. Then the disciples were overjoyed when they saw the master.
>
> "Peace be with you," Jesus said to them again. "As the father has sent me, so I'm sending you."
>
> With that, he breathed on them.
>
> "Receive the holy spirit," he said. "if you forgive anyone's sins, they are forgiven. if you retain anyone's sins, they are retained" (John 20:19–23).

> One of the Twelve, Thomas (also known as Didymus), wasn't with them when Jesus came. So the other disciples spoke to him.
>
> "We've seen the master!" they said.
>
> "Unless I see the mark of the nails in his hands," replied Thomas, "and put my finger into the nail-marks, and put my hand into his side—I'm not going to believe!"
>
> A week later the disciples were again in the house, and Thomas was with them. The doors were shut. Jesus came and stood in the middle of them.
>
> "Peace be with you!" he said. Then he addressed Thomas. "Bring your finger here," he said, "and inspect my hands. Bring your hand here and put it into my side. Don't be faithless! Just believe!"

"My Lord," replied Thomas, "and my God!"

"Is it because you've seen me that you believe?" replied Jesus. "God's blessing on people who don't see, and yet believe!"

Jesus did many other signs in the presence of his disciples, which aren't written in this book. But these are written so that you may believe that the Messiah, the son of God, is none other than Jesus; and that, with this faith, you may have life in his name (John 20:24–30).

What did these people experience in their encounter with the risen Messiah? How did the encounter influence their belief that Jesus was truly raised from the dead?

6. Jesus not only rose from the dead and ascended to heaven but is also alive today and working in our lives. What is a real and personal way the risen Jesus has empowered you, guided you, or protected you? How does the present work of Jesus in your life and your world affirm the reality of his resurrection?

The Immediate Implications of the Resurrection

From the start, the implications of the resurrection for the disciples was that God's new creation had begun. Somehow, God had dealt with the fact of death itself in the person of Jesus. As the disciples reflected on that truth over the weeks and months that followed, they realized the ancient texts they had known and loved since their childhood had been fulfilled . . . but in a completely unexpected way.

7. Read the following teaching from Paul on baptism and the resurrection:

> What are we to say, then? Shall we continue in the state of sin, so that grace may increase? Certainly not! We died to sin; how can we still live in it? Don't you know that all of us who were baptized into the Messiah, Jesus, were baptized into his death? That means that we were buried with him, through baptism, into death, so that, just as the Messiah was raised from the dead through the father's glory, we too might behave with a new quality of life. For if we have been planted together in the likeness of his death, we shall also be in the likeness of his resurrection.
>
> This is what we know: our old humanity was crucified with the Messiah, so that the bodily solidarity of sin might be abolished, and that we should no longer be enslaved to sin. A person who has died, you see, has been declared free from all charges of sin.
>
> But if we died with the Messiah, we believe that we shall live with him. We know that the Messiah, having been raised from the dead, will never die again. Death no longer has any authority over him. The death he died, you see, he died to sin, once and only once. But the life he lives, he lives to God. In the same way you, too, must calculate yourselves as being dead to sin, and alive to God in the Messiah, Jesus (Romans 6:1–11).

The church, from its inception to this day, has been driven by a belief in the life, death, and resurrection of our Messiah. How is baptism a powerful picture of the resurrection power of Jesus being unleashed in the life of a believer?

8. Read the following powerful and hope-filled passage on the resurrection:

> This is what I'm saying, my dear family. Flesh and blood can't inherit God's kingdom; decay can't inherit undecaying life. Look! I'm telling you a mystery. We won't all sleep; we're all going to be changed—in a flash, at the blink of an eye, at the last trumpet. This is how it will be, you see: the trumpet's going to sound, the dead will be raised undecaying, and we're going to be changed. This decaying body must put on the undecaying one; this dying body must put on deathlessness. When the decaying puts on the undecaying, and the dying puts on the undying, then the saying that has been written will come true:
>
> Death is swallowed up in victory! Death, where's your victory gone? Death, where's your sting gone?
>
> The "sting" of death is sin, and the power of sin is the law. But thank God! He gives us the victory, through our Lord Jesus the Messiah.
>
> So, my dear family, be firmly fixed, unshakable, always full to overflowing with the Lord's work. In the Lord, as you know, the work you're doing will not be worthless (1 Corinthians 15:50–58).

What hope does this passage promise for those who choose to follow Jesus and put their faith in the resurrected Messiah?

The Ultimate Weapon Removed

Death was the ultimate weapon of the tyrant in Jesus' day. The Romans (and others) ruled by bullying, by fear, and by cudgeling people. The people understood that if they didn't do what the tyrant said, he would make life very bad for them. But the resurrection says the living God has a weapon that goes beyond death—and this ultimately removes the tyrant's power.

CLOSING PRAYER

Take time as a group to pray in some of the following directions . . .

- Thank God that Jesus rose from the dead and that he promises to raise us up as well if we place our faith in him.
- Ask Jesus to give you a fresh new perspective on his resurrection and what it means for your life today and for eternity.
- Thank God that the tomb is empty, Jesus is alive, and his power has been unleashed in your life and the world.
- Pray that the resurrected Jesus would draw near to the group members, help them, fill them, and empower them at their point of need.

SESSION 4

Between-Sessions Personal Study

Reflect on the content you've covered this week in *The New Testament You Never Knew* by engaging in any or all of the following between-sessions activities. The time you invest will be well spent, so let God use it to draw you closer to him. At your next meeting, share with your group any key points or insights that stood out to you as you spent this time with the Lord.

REFLECTION

How do the accounts of the empty tomb increase your confidence and certainty of Jesus' resurrection?

How do the many post-resurrection appearances give you assurance that Jesus truly rose from the dead?

How have you encountered the resurrected Jesus in the course of your life? How has this given you confidence that Jesus is risen and reigns over the universe?

Write a prayer asking Jesus to fill you with his resurrection today so you can live more passionately and more fully for him.

STUDY

Commit to spending some time this week to read the following passages from the Old Testament, which offer glimmers and hints of resurrection. Think about how these passages might have been re-read by the early Christians after the resurrection of Jesus.

Day 1: 1 Kings 17

What you learned about resurrection . . .

Day 2: 2 Kings 4

What you learned about resurrection . . .

Day 3: Psalm 16

What you learned about resurrection . . .

Day 4: Isaiah 26

What you learned about resurrection . . .

Day 5: Daniel 12

What you learned about resurrection . . .

RESPONSE

For the entire history of the church, Christians have rejoiced in the reality that everything has been made new through the resurrection of Jesus. This week, make a list of (1) what God has made new, and (2) what he is still making new in your life. Then lift up prayers to celebrate what he has done and ask for the completion of what he still wants to do in you.

God Has Made Things New

Make a list of things you have seen God make new in your own life . . .

Lift up prayers of praise, thanks, and adoration to God for these things he has done through his resurrection power.

God Is Still Making Things New

Make a list of things you want to see God transform and make new in your life . . .

Lift up prayers asking Jesus to unleash his power in your life, the lives of the people you love, your church, your community, and the world. Ask for the specific things you listed above.

APPLICATION

The reality of Jesus' resurrection defined the lives of the early believers and gave them a new purpose as a community. The same is true in our world today. Think about how the resurrection of Christ impacts and guides:

The life and behavior of someone who wants to grow as a disciple of the Messiah . . .

The way in which believers gather for worship . . .

The overall mission of the church . . .

FOR NEXT WEEK

Use the space below to write any key insights or questions from your personal study that you want to discuss at the next group meeting.

THE MINISTRY OF THE APOSTLE PAUL

Everything for Paul changed when he met Jesus on the road to Damascus. Suddenly, he realized that even though it had seemed impossible before, a crucified man who had claimed to be Messiah had been vindicated by Israel's God, the creator God. And with that realization came a new call, a new vocation, to take that message to the ends of the earth.

N.T. WRIGHT

INTRODUCTION

Imagine a team of leaders sitting around a table with a specific task to accomplish. They have to recruit, hire, and empower a new CEO for a large non-profit Christian ministry with the mission of *creatively expanding the impact and reach of the gospel of Jesus all over the world*. This group has limited resources but a massive vision. As the leaders talk, they come up with a list of characteristics they think would be important for this new CEO to possess:

- A deep and personal love for God and a rich spiritual life rooted in a personal encounter with the Savior.
- Passion for the mission of extending the impact of the gospel.
- Personal integrity and a commitment to speaking the truth— even when that truth is difficult and painful for others to hear.
- An ability to effectively communicate both verbally and in writing.
- A strong educational background and academic pedigree.
- A deep and personal sense of call to follow and serve Jesus.
- An understanding of his or her own culture and the culture of others.
- A tenacious personality and relentless drive to never quit.
- Love for people—both in the faith and those who are far from Jesus.
- An ability to set trends—to know tradition but not be bound by it.
- An ability to relate well with both insiders and outsiders.
- A desire to disciple and raise up the next generation of men and women who will also share in the ministry.

As the group of leaders look at this list of desired qualities and attributes, they realize it would be highly unlikely for them to find any *one person* who possessed all of these traits. They would likely narrow the list to their top six attributes. They would then try to find a CEO who would hit as many of those key markers as possible.

However, when God decided to recruit a leader for the early church, he found someone who hit *all* of these key character traits. God picked Saul of Tarsus—a man who had previously persecuted the church—to be the leader who would move the movement beyond the almost exclusively Jewish converts into the Gentile world. The apostle Paul, as he would later become known, had the necessary skills to understand and interact with people from not only his own Jewish background but also those in the Greco-Roman world.

God knew the essential nature of the task that needed to be done. So he chose a leader who was up for both the exhilarating highs and painful lows of leading the early church into the world with the message of the risen Messiah.

The Impact of the Apostle Paul

Paul the apostle, the traveler, the Roman citizen, the letter writer, and the theologian is the one who invented something we can call Christian theology. In Paul we have a man who not only left his mark on the church but also shaped a movement that would eventually subsume the Roman empire and even change the course of western civilization.

TALK ABOUT IT

Welcome to the fifth session of *The New Testament You Never Knew*. To get things started, discuss one of the following questions as a group:

- If you had to pick just four of the characteristics on the list you just read of traits important for a new CEO to possess, which would you choose? Why those particular characteristics?

—*or*—

- Based on what you know about the apostle Paul, how do you see one or two of these characteristics playing out in his life and ministry?

VIDEO TEACHING NOTES

Play the video segment for session five. As you watch, use the space provided to collect your thoughts and make some notes about the New Testament that are new and fresh for you.

The Uniqueness of Paul

Paul's early life and the moment that changed everything

Paul's unique attributes that allowed him to spread the message of Christ

Paul's Use of Scripture

"[Paul] spent years of his life on the road, carrying (presumably on pack animals) his tent, clothing and tools—not many scrolls, if any. He carried the Bible safely tucked away in his head, where it belongs."*

Paul's View of the God of Israel

The religions and culture of the world in which Paul travelled

How Paul redefined the identity of Israel's God

---

* E.P. Sanders, "Did Paul's Theology Develop?" in *The Word Leaps the Gap: Essays on Scripture and Theology in Honor of Richard B. Hays*, eds. J. Ross Wagner, C. Kavin Rowe, and A. Katherine Grieb (Grand Rapids, Mich: Eerdmans, 2008), 347.

Who Jesus Is for Paul

Robert M. Bowman and J. Ed Komoszewski use the following "HANDS" acronym (cited in the video teaching) to describe how in Paul's view, Jesus: shared the Honors of God, the Attributes of God, the Names of God, did the Deeds of God, and even shared God's Seat (or throne).*

Paul's View of the People of God

The role of the Messiah in defining the people of God

Paul's view of who comprised the true children of Abraham

Paul's View of Jesus as Lord

The imperial cult and its implication for Christians

Paul's view of earthly authorities

Paul and the Doctrine of Justification

Justification and the unity of the church

---

* Robert M. Bowman and J. Ed Komoszewski, *Putting Jesus in His Place: The Case for the Deity of Christ* (Grand Rapids. Mich: Kregel, 2007).

Justification and eschatology (the end of time)

The Doctrine of Justification

At the heart of the doctrine of justification is the idea that God intends to put the whole world right in the end. God launched that project by raising Jesus from the dead, and he now makes us right through the death and resurrection of Jesus and the work of the Holy Spirit in our lives. As he does this, we become part of his putting-right project in and for the world.

GROUP DISCUSSION

Take a few minutes to discuss what you just watched and explore these concepts together.

1. Why was Paul seen as such a controversial figure by both the Jewish religious leaders and the Roman authorities? Why were many of their concerns actually valid?

2. Read the following passages from Paul about God being one:

   There is one body and one spirit; you were, after all, called to one hope which goes with your call. There is one Lord, one faith, one baptism; one God and father of all, who is over all, through all, and in all (Ephesians 4:4–6).

So when it comes to food that has been offered to idols, we know that "idols are nothing in the world," and that "there is no God but one." Yes, indeed: there may be many so-called "gods," whether in heaven or on earth, just as there are many "gods" and many "lords." But for us

> There is one God, the father,
> From whom are all things, and we live to him and for him;
> And one Lord, Jesus the Messiah,
> Through whom are all things, and we live through him
>   (1 Corinthians 8:4–6).

How does Paul show that he is uncompromisingly committed to the declaration there is only one God? What would be the implications if Paul had embraced a polytheistic world view (which was popular in the culture of his day)?

3. Read the following passages from Paul about the divinity of Jesus:

This is how you should think among yourselves—with the mind that you have because you belong to the Messiah, Jesus:

> Who, though in God's form, did not
> Regard his equality with God
> As something he ought to exploit.
> Instead, he emptied himself,
> And received the form of a slave,
> Being born in the likeness of humans.
> And then, having human appearance,
> He humbled himself, and became
> Obedient even to death,
> Yes, even the death of the cross.
> And so God has greatly exalted him,
> And to him in his favor has given
> The name which is over all names:
> That now at the name of Jesus

Every knee within heaven shall bow—
On earth, too, and under the earth;
And every tongue shall confess
That Jesus, Messiah, is Lord,
To the glory of God, the father (Philippians 2:5–11).

He is the one in whom we have redemption, the forgiveness of sins.

He is the image of God, the invisible one,
    The firstborn of all creation.
For in him all things were created,
    In the heavens and here on the earth.
Things we can see and things we cannot—
    Thrones and lordships and rulers and powers—
All things were created both through him and for him.

And he is ahead, prior to all else,
    And in him all things hold together;
And he himself is supreme, the head
    Over the body, the church.

He is the start of it all,
    Firstborn from realms of the dead;
    So in all things he might be the chief.
For in him all the Fullness was glad to dwell
    And through him to reconcile all to himself,
    Making peace through the blood of his cross,
Through him—yes, things on the earth,
    And also the things in the heavens
    (Colossians 1:14–20).

Though there is only one God, he exists in three persons, and each of these persons is fully God. How do these passages affirm and unfold the full divinity of Jesus? How have you experienced Jesus as the God who is with you?

Paul's Monotheism

Paul was a Jew who believed in one God, the God of creation, the God of covenant. He could say the Shema from Deuteronomy 6:4: "Hear, O Israel: The LORD is our God, the LORD alone." And yet, Paul believed this one God had been revealed in Jesus Christ. Paul was absolutely devoted to Jesus, but he never lost sight of the oneness of God.

4. Read the following teaching from Paul about the family of God:

So I ask, then: Have they tripped up in such a way as to fall completely? Certainly not! Rather, by their trespass, salvation has come to the nations, in order to make them jealous. If their trespass means riches for the world, and their impoverishment means riches for the nations, how much more will their fullness mean!

Now I am speaking to you Gentiles. Insofar as I am the apostle of the Gentiles, I celebrate my particular ministry, so that, if possible, I can make my "flesh" jealous, and save some of them. If their casting away, you see, means reconciliation for the world, what will their acceptance mean but life from the dead?

Take another illustration: if the first fruits are holy, so is the whole lump.

And another: if the root is holy, so are the branches.

But if some of the branches were broken off, and you—a wild olive tree!—were grafted in among them, and came to share in the root of the olive with its rich sap, don't boast over the branches. If you do boast, remember this: it isn't you that supports the root, but the root that supports you.

I know what you'll say next: "Branches were broken off so that I could be grafted in." That's all very well. They were broken off because of unbelief—but you stand firm by faith. Don't get big ideas about it; instead, be afraid. After all, if God didn't spare the natural branches, there's a strong possibility he won't spare you.

Note carefully, then, that God is both kind and severe. He is severe to those who have fallen, but he is kind to you, provided you continue in his kindness—otherwise you too will be cut off. And they, too, if they do not remain in unbelief, will be grafted back in. God is able, you see, to graft them back in. For if you were cut out of what is by nature a wild olive tree, and grafted, contrary to nature, into a cultivated olive tree, how much more will they, the natural branches, be grafted back into their own olive tree (Romans 11:11–24).

What does Paul teach in this passage about who can be part of God's family? What does he teach about what the community of God's people actually looks like?

5. Read the following passage from Paul about submitting to governing authorities:

Every person must be subject to the ruling authorities. There is no authority, you see, except from God, and those that exist have been put in place by God. As a result, anyone who rebels against authority is resisting what God has set up, and those who resist will bring judgment on themselves. For rulers hold no terrors for people who do good, but only for people who do evil.

If you want to have no fear of the ruling power, do what is good, and it will praise you. It is God's servant, you see, for you and your good. But if you do evil, be afraid; the sword it carries is no empty gesture. It is God's servant, you see: an agent of justice to bring his anger on evildoers. That is why it is necessary to submit, not only to avoid punishment but because of conscience.

That, too, is why you pay taxes. The officials in question are God's ministers, attending to this very thing. So pay each of them what is owed: tribute to those who collect it, revenue to those who collect it. Respect those who should be respected. Honor the people one ought to honor (Romans 13:1–7).

What did Paul teach about a Christian's responsibility as a citizen? Why is it important for followers of Jesus to be reminded of this in every generation?

6. Although Paul calls believers to honor governing authorities, it is clear he understood that government and civic servants are under the power, rule, and hand of God. How do you see this emphasized in the passage from Romans? What does this teach about our devotion to God above all human powers and authorities?

Jesus or Political Leaders?

The reason the emperor Nero sent Christians to the lions was not because they said Jesus was the Lord of their heart but because they said Jesus was Lord of all. They gave absolute sovereignty to Jesus over the areas of life typically claimed by Caesar. When we read the New Testament, what rises to the surface is the question of who is the ruler of all. It comes down to one of two options: Is it the emperor? Or is it Jesus the Messiah?

7. Read the following passage from Paul about justification and unity in the church:

> We are Jews by birth, not "Gentile sinners." But we know that a person is not declared "righteous" by works of the Jewish law, but through the faithfulness of Jesus the Messiah.
>
> That is why we too believed in the Messiah, Jesus: so that we might be declared "righteous" on the basis of the Messiah's faithfulness, and not on the basis of works of the Jewish law. On that basis, you see, no creature will be declared "righteous."
>
> Well, then; if, in seeking to be declared "righteous" in the Messiah, we ourselves are found to be "sinners," does that make the Messiah an agent of "sin"? Certainly not! If I build up once more the things which I tore down, I demonstrate that I am a lawbreaker.
>
> Let me explain it like this. Through the law I died to the law, so that I might live to God. I have been crucified with the Messiah. I am, however, alive—but it isn't me any longer; it's the Messiah who lives in me. And the life I do still live in the flesh, I live within the faithfulness of the son of God, who loved me and gave himself for me (Galatians 2:15–20).

What justifies Jews and Gentiles and unites them into one family? What does Paul warn about trying to earn one's way into a justified relationship with God and others?

8. Read the following personal reflection from Paul:

> Does that sound as though my account was well in credit? Well, maybe; but whatever I had written in on the profit side, I calculated it instead as a loss—because of the Messiah. Yes, I know that's weird, but there's more: I calculate everything as a loss, because knowing King Jesus as my Lord is worth far more than everything else put together! In fact, because of the Messiah I've suffered the loss of everything, and I now calculate it as trash, so that my profit may be the Messiah, and that I may be discovered in him, not having my own covenant status defined by Torah, but the status which comes through the Messiah's faithfulness: the covenant status from God which is given to faith. This means knowing him, knowing the power of his resurrection, and knowing the partnership of his sufferings. It means sharing the form and pattern of his death, so that somehow I may arrive at the final resurrection from the dead (Philippians 3:7–11).

An important part of Paul's teaching on justification is that Jesus transforms us and justifies us through his sacrifice. What do you learn from this teaching about the attitude and lifestyle a Christian should possess? What are some specific ways you can adopt this kind of attitude and change your actions to line up with this teaching?

What Is the Church?

The church is a community of people living together in a way that is radically different from the people around them. For Paul, the big symbol is the people who belong to Jesus. One can tell who these people are because they live under his lordship and bear his cross.

CLOSING PRAYER

Take time as a group to pray in some of the following directions . . .

- Thank God for the Christian leaders who have influenced your life of faith.
- Ask God to help you to be willing to suffer for his sake, if doing so will extend his kingdom.
- Lift up people in your life who have still not been justified through the work of Jesus on the cross.
- Lift up prayers of praise and adoration to Jesus as God, the divine one.
- Pray for the leaders in your local church to grow in and exhibit character that honors God, reflects Jesus, and blesses the people in the congregation.

Between-Sessions Personal Study

Reflect on the content you've covered this week in *The New Testament You Never Knew* by engaging in any or all of the following between-sessions activities. The time you invest will be well spent, so let God use it to draw you closer to him. At your next meeting, share with your group any key points or insights that stood out to you as you spent this time with the Lord.

REFLECTION

What qualities and characteristics do you want God to grow in you over the coming year to make you a more influential person of Jesus?

How is God calling you to be different and even to suffer for the sake of his name?

In what ways do you need to increase your commitment to follow the governing authorities while still holding Jesus above all other influences in your life?

Write a prayer for your pastor (or pastors) and other leaders in your church. Pray for God's protection and leading in their lives and for them to grow in Christlikeness.

STUDY

Commit to spending some time this week to study the following teachings from Paul on justification and how sinful people are made righteous in God's sight.

Day 1: Romans 4–6

What you learned about justification . . .

Day 2: Romans 9–11

What you learned about justification . . .

Day 3: Galatians 2–3

What you learned about justification . . .

Day 4: Ephesians 1

What you learned about justification . . .

Day 5: Philippians 3

What you learned about justification . . .

RESPONSE

Take time this week to study Paul's ministry journey in the book of Acts. Read Acts 13–14 and 16–19 and write down five key insights you learn about (1) following Jesus, (2) counting the cost, and (3) sharing the message of the risen Messiah.

Insight #1

Insight #2

Insight #3

Insight #4

Insight #5

APPLICATION

At the beginning of this session you read a list of characteristics that make a good leader . . . all of which we find in Paul. Identify three of these traits you want to develop in your life, and then identify one or two action steps that will help you grow this quality in your life.

Characteristic #1:

What you will begin doing to develop this characteristic . . .

How you will pray . . .

Who will cheer you on and keep you accountable . . .

Characteristic #2:

What you will begin doing to develop this characteristic . . .

How you will pray . . .

Who will cheer you on and keep you accountable . . .

Characteristic #3:

What you will begin doing to develop this characteristic . . .

How you will pray . . .

Who will cheer you on and keep you accountable . . .

FOR NEXT WEEK

Use the space below to write any key insights or questions from your personal study that you want to discuss at the next group meeting.

THE EARLY CHRISTIANS AND THE CHURCH

At the end of the day, the early Christians believed they were the ones on whom the end of the ages had come. They believed in Israel's Messiah. They could receive the Spirit. They were a people of the Word, of Spirit, and of sacrament, believing God had a plan for this world that would begin with them and would come to fruition through them.

MICHAEL F. BIRD

INTRODUCTION

Throughout the years, many little church-going boys and girls have been taught a simple little poem with hand movements. Maybe you know it. The words are memorable:

> This is the church,
> Here is the steeple,
> Open the door,
> See all the people!

The song is clever. It rhymes. It is cute. But it is bad theology! This little poem gives the impression that the church is a building that houses a bunch of people. And we hear comments all the time from people that reinforce the same idea.

Of course, we know the church is so much more than just a location or a structure—regardless of how impressive that building may be. The New Testament teaches the church is the people of God. It is the community of Jesus-followers gathered together.

The early Christians did not have big or fancy buildings. While some might have met in the lavish homes of a wealthy member, others met in squalid apartments, or outdoors, or in community buildings, or any number of other places. What made them unique was not where they met but who they were. Their beliefs set them apart and made them distinct.

The church existed long before the advent of mega-churches, building campaigns, formal and liturgical worship services, and the various denominations we see today. In the New Testament times—as today—the church represents the people of God. We are followers of the King, the risen Messiah, the Savior.

We are the church.

The Mission of the Early Church

The often risky and costly mission of the early church can only be explained in terms of the belief that the God of Israel had acted in Jesus to redeem Israel—and a redeemed Israel would transform the world. Israel's Messiah had inaugurated a new covenant, and through his death and resurrection, God's never-failing love would reach out to the whole world.

TALK ABOUT IT

Welcome to the sixth session of *The New Testament You Never Knew*. To get things started, discuss one of the following questions as a group:

- When you think about the church, what images, experiences, or memories come to mind? Why?

—*or*—

- Why is it easy to think of the church as just a location where believers meet at a set time? Why is it important to expand this understanding of the church?

VIDEO TEACHING NOTES

Play the video segment for session six. As you watch, use the space provided to collect your thoughts and make some notes about the New Testament that are new and fresh for you.

Early Church Society

Christians seen by outsiders as a strange and eclectic group

Early Church Beliefs

Christians were monotheists of the Jewish type

Christians believed in a single story

Christians viewed themselves as one family

Christians believed in personal holiness

How the Early Christians Were Viewed

Toward the end of the second century AD, the pagan doctor Galen wrote about the "Nazarenes." He only knew two things about them, but these two things were striking. One was that they believed in the resurrection of the body, and the other was that they didn't sleep around. Galen thought they were mad on both accounts, for he didn't know anyone else who had those two particular beliefs as part of their worldview. These sorts of traits made the Christians distinctive.

Christians in the Jewish World (the Epistle of James)

The reality of persecution and scattering

A strong anticipation of what God will do in the future

Christians in the Roman World (1 Corinthians)

The challenge of navigating what it means to follow Jesus in a pagan society

Warnings against divisions and personality cults in the church

Issues of morality and questions about the resurrection

The Struggle of the Early Christians

The life of the early church was a matter of believers struggling to be loyal to Jesus while the world was pulling them in different directions. God was teaching them through leaders like Paul to think in a new way . . . to think "Christianly." The early believers had to learn what it meant to be loyal to Jesus in all areas of life both before the watching world and within the hostile world.

GROUP DISCUSSION

Take a few minutes to discuss what you just watched and explore these concepts together.

1. What was the main message of the church during the first century? What was the primary message you heard in the church where you grew up? What message do you think the church *should* be communicating to the world?

2. Read the following passage about Jesus' death, resurrection, and the meaning of baptism:

> Don't you know that all of us who were baptized into the Messiah, Jesus, were baptized into his death? That means that we were buried with him, through baptism, into death, so that, just as the Messiah was raised from the dead through the father's glory, we too might behave with a new quality of life. For if we have been planted together in the likeness of his death, we shall also be in the likeness of his resurrection.
>
> This is what we know: our old humanity was crucified with the Messiah, so that the bodily solidarity of sin might be abolished, and that we should no longer be enslaved to sin. A person who has died, you see, has been declared free from all charges of sin.
>
> But if we died with the Messiah, we believe that we shall live with him (Romans 6:3–8).

How does Christian baptism build on the Old Testament imagery of the Israelites coming through the Jordan River into the Promised Land? How is baptism a sign of dying with Christ and also being raised with him?

The Symbolism of Baptism

When John started baptizing people on the banks of the Jordan River, he was doing something filled with symbolism. Baptism was a picture of the Israelites coming out of Egypt through the waters of the Red Sea and then into the Promised Land through the Jordan River. John was thus announcing the kingdom of God was coming like a new exodus. Jesus later chose Passover—the exodus moment—to complete his work on the cross. For this reason, baptism came to symbolize both the old exodus and the "new" exodus—the death and resurrection of Christ.

3. Read the following snapshot regarding some of the behaviors of the early church:

> All of those who believed came together, and held everything in common. They sold their possessions and belongings and divided them up to everyone in proportion to their various needs. Day by day they were all together attending the Temple. They broke bread in their various houses, and ate their food with glad and sincere hearts, praising God and standing in favor with all the people. And every day the Lord added to their number those who were being rescued (Acts 2:44–47).

What were some of the practices of the early Christians? How do we model these same behaviors? What are ways we can embrace these even more firmly?

4. Read the following passages written by James about persecution and suffering:

> My dear family, when you find yourselves tumbling into various trials and tribulations, learn to look at it with complete joy, because you know that, when your faith is put to the test, what comes out is patience. What's more, you must let patience have its complete effect, so that you may be complete and whole, not falling short in anything (James 1:2–4).

> God's blessing on the man who endures testing! When he has passed the test, he will receive the crown of life, which God has promised to those who love him (James 1:12).

> Consider the prophets, my brothers and sisters, who spoke in the name of the Lord. Take them as an example of long-suffering and patience. When people endure, we call them "blessed by God." Well, you have heard of the endurance of Job; and you saw the Lord's ultimate purpose. The Lord is deeply compassionate and kindly (James 5:10–11).

How can persecution, struggles, and suffering actually deepen and strengthen a person's faith? How have you experienced this spiritual reality?

Persecution and the Early Church

The Jerusalem church went through a series of persecutions. We know from Acts there was a persecution during the early 40s, at which time the disciple James was put to death for his faith. Josephus, the Jewish historian, tells us James the brother of Jesus was put to death sometime around AD 62. According to tradition, the Jerusalem Christians fled Jerusalem on the eve of the Jewish revolt, sometime around AD 66. They traveled north to the Trans-Jordan region to avoid these attacks. Persecution and suffering were part of following Jesus in the ancient world.

5. Read the following passage from Paul about conflicts in the early church:

> Now I must appeal to you, my brothers and sisters, through the name of King Jesus our Lord, that you should all be in agreement, and that there should be no divisions among you. Instead, you should be fully equipped with the same mind and the same opinion.
>
> You see, my dear family, Chloe's people have put me in the picture about you—about the fact that you are having quarrels. What I'm talking about is this. Each one of you is saying, "I'm with Paul!" "I'm with Apollos!" "I'm with Cephas!" "I'm with the Messiah!" Well! Has the Messiah been cut up into pieces? Was Paul crucified for you? Or were you baptized into Paul's name? (1 Corinthians 1:10–13).

Why is it dangerous for Christians to be devoted to a pastor, leader, or even a specific congregation above their commitment to follow Jesus? What can we do to avoid "personality cults" in the church and make sure our eyes are fixed only on Jesus?

6. Read the following passages from Paul about fleeing from sexual immorality:

> Everybody's talking about the sex scandal that's going on in your community, not least because it's a kind of immorality that even the pagans don't practice! Well I never—a man taking his father's wife! And you're puffed up! Why aren't you in mourning? Why aren't you getting rid of the person who's done such a thing? (1 Corinthians 5:1–2).

> Don't you know that your bodies are members of the Messiah? Shall I then take the members of the Messiah and make them members of a prostitute? Of course not! Or don't you know that anyone who joins himself to a prostitute is one body with her? "The two shall become one flesh"—that's what it says. But the one who joins himself to the Lord becomes one spirit with him.
>
> Run away from immorality. Every sin that it's possible for someone to commit happens outside the body; but immorality involves sinning against your own body. Or don't you know that your body is a temple of the holy spirit within you, the spirit God gave you, so that you don't belong to yourselves? You were quite an expensive purchase! So glorify God in your body (1 Corinthians 6:15–20).

What were some of the sexual sins and struggles the early church faced? Why does Paul say it is critical for believers in Christ to flee from sexual immorality?

7. One of the unique attributes of Jesus' people is that they seek to live and grow in holiness. What are some of the holy choices Christians make that don't make sense to the world around them? How can your group members pray for you as you seek to live a holy life that is guided by the resurrected Messiah?

8. Read the following passage from Paul about the resurrection of believers:

> Now concerning those who have fallen asleep: we don't want you to remain in ignorance about them, my dear family. We don't want you to have the kind of grief that other people do, people who don't have any hope. For, you see, if we believe that Jesus died and rose, that's the way God will also, through Jesus, bring with him those who have fallen asleep.
>
> Let me explain. (This is the word of the Lord I'm speaking to you!) We who are alive, who remain until the Lord is present, will not find ourselves ahead of those who fell asleep. The Lord himself will come down from heaven with a shouted order, with the voice of an archangel and the sound of God's trumpet. The Messiah's dead will rise first; then we who are alive, who are left, will be snatched up with them among the clouds, to meet the Lord in the air. And in this way we shall always be with the Lord. So comfort each other with these words (1 Thessalonians 4:13–18).

For followers of the Christ, death is not the end of the story but the real beginning. How can living with confidence that your story will end in heaven bring you hope, confidence, or strength today? When was a time your confidence in God's sovereignty over your life story helped you to make it through a hard time?

How the Early Christians Viewed Themselves

The early Christians believed in the one God. They believed in the Messiah. They believed in covenant and creation. And yet they believed this had all come to a climax in the Messiah. They had received the Spirit . . . they were the beneficiaries . . . they were the recipients of the promises of Israel. They organized their lives around that belief, that hope, and that story. For the early believers, this was an exciting new thing they had received, and they were determined to live as Christians—while still getting muddled at times about what that actually meant.

CLOSING PRAYER

Take time as a group to pray in some of the following directions . . .

- Thank God for the people you have encountered in the church who have loved you and taught you the faith.
- Pray for yourself and for your fellow church members to grow in your understanding of what it means to really be part of the family of God.
- Ask God to help you walk in unity with Christians in your congregation and followers of Jesus who are part of other congregations in your community.
- Lift up praise that Jesus will one day come again and acknowledge that he holds history and your life in his hands.
- Confess where you are prone to show favoritism and ask God to help you love all people in the name of Jesus.
- Pray for unity among believers and ask God to make you an agent of peace.

Between-Sessions Personal Study

Reflect on the content you've covered this week in *The New Testament You Never Knew* by engaging in any or all of the following between-sessions activities. The time you invest will be well spent, so let God use it to draw you closer to him. At your next meeting, share with your group any key points or insights that stood out to you as you spent this time with the Lord.

REFLECTION

What does baptism mean to you? Does your understanding reflect the deep and rich meaning God has given to this powerful experience?

What does communion (the Lord's Supper) mean to you? How can you grow in your understanding of this sacrament and experience it in more meaningful ways?

What does it mean to walk and live in holiness? How can you grow to be more attentive to your own growth in holiness?

Write down a prayer for the people in your church. Ask God to protect them, lead them, and work through them. Pray they will not be divided but will look to Jesus and focus on him alone.

STUDY

Commit to spending some time this week to read the following passages from the book of 1 Corinthians. Seek to learn from this church's challenges, struggles, and outright points of sin. Take note of the issues this church faced as they dealt with the complexities of doing life together. Identify ways Paul's advice can shape how you live in community with God's people.

Day 1: 1 Corinthians 1–3

Issues the church faced as they dealt with the complexities of doing life together . . .

How Paul's advice can shape how you live in community . . .

Day 2: 1 Corinthians 4–6

Issues the church faced as they dealt with the complexities of doing life together . . .

How Paul's advice can shape how you live in community . . .

Day 3: 1 Corinthians 7–10

Issues the church faced as they dealt with the complexities of doing life together . . .

How Paul's advice can shape how you live in community . . .

Day 4: 1 Corinthians 11–13

Issues the church faced as they dealt with the complexities of doing life together . . .

How Paul's advice can shape how you live in community . . .

Day 5: 1 Corinthians 14–16

Issues the church faced as they dealt with the complexities of doing life together . . .

How Paul's advice can shape how you live in community . . .

RESPONSE

We all have pastors we love, preachers we respect, and Christians we know who have had a great impact on our lives. This is good and it is a gift. The danger comes when our devotion to these people causes us to forget they are imperfect people. Take time today to think of three Christians you hold in high regard. In the space below, write down the person's name and why you respect him or her. Then write down a prayer for that person, asking God to bless their faithfulness, protect their life and ministry, and anything else that comes to mind.

Person #1:

Why you respect him or her:

Your prayer for this person . . .

Person #2:

Why you respect him or her:

Your prayer for this person . . .

Person #3:

Why you respect him or her:

Your prayer for this person . . .

APPLICATION

Reflect on these words from Jesus found in Matthew 18:15–17:

> If another disciple sins against you . . . go and have it out, just between the two of you alone. If they listen to you, you've won back a brother or sister. But if they won't listen, you should take with you one or two others, so that "everything may be established from the mouth of two or three witnesses." If they won't listen to them, tell it to the assembly. And if they won't listen to the assembly, you should treat such a person like you would a Gentile or a tax-collector.

> If you are comfortable in doing so, write down the names of one or two people with whom you have experienced conflict and have not yet had reconciliation in the relationship.

Person #1: _____

Person #2: _____

Commit to walk through Jesus' instructions in the passage and take the actions God calls you to take. If you are not sure how to move forward, talk with your pastor or another leader in your church. (Be sure not to share the specifics or the name of the person unless you are at the second or third step and need the pastor or leader to go with you.)

FOR NEXT WEEK

Use the space below to write any key insights or questions from your personal study that you want to discuss at the next group meeting.

THE MISSION OF THE CHURCH

The early Christians did not simply say that Jesus was somebody who could help people out of their present mess and maybe help them get away from this earth altogether to a place called heaven. Rather, they were planting signs of new creation within the world as it is, so that in the power of the resurrection and in the fresh wind of the Spirit, God would be at work to transform people's lives and people's societies.

N.T. WRIGHT

INTRODUCTION

Most people who drive a car have a basic sense of how their vehicle works. They put in gas when the gauge gets near empty. If they are wise, they get regular tune-ups. They drive with responsibility, signal before changing lanes, stop at red lights, and follow the posted rules of the road. Cars are not that complicated . . . until something stops working. Most car owners discover just how little they really know about their car when the engine sputters and stops on the side of a road in the middle of nowhere. In a traumatic moment, they pop the hood, look at their engine, and realize they have no idea how this machine really works.

The same is true of smartphones. It seems as if everyone on the planet has one. Even young children know how to open apps on Dad's or Mom's device and play games, look at pictures, and make a call. Kids today, at younger and younger ages, are able to navigate the digital world with these small handheld devices. But let's be honest—almost no one has any idea how these handheld mini computers actually work. We can't write code or repair a crashed system. The complexity of these devices is far greater than we realize.

Or consider a couple who stands at the altar on their wedding day. Both of them have a sense they know their spouse. After all, they would not be getting married if they did not have some sense they knew who the person was and what made him or her tick. But even after thirty years, if you were to ask the simple question as to whether they have the other person figured out, both would likely say no. An honest husband might say something like, "I love her, I understand her more with each passing year, but I am not sure I will ever totally figure her out!" A truthful wife would say something very similar. People are complex, and time teaches us not only what we know but also what we still have to learn.

Likewise, if you were to ask a Christian to describe what is the gospel and what is the mission of the church, many would have an answer for you. It would likely be short, sweet, and reflect something they learned in Sunday School or heard in a sermon. In most cases, the answer would be true or mostly true . . . but not a fully-orbed and theologically sound understanding of these massive and complex spiritual realities.

The mission of the church and the gospel of Jesus Christ are more complex than we realize. At first glance, they seem simple and straightforward, like driving a car, using a smart phone, or getting married. Yet when we look a little closer, we discover there is richness and complexity that undergird these core elements of the New Testament church and our lives as followers of Christ.

So let's pop the hood and take a closer look!

A Missional Community

The church has always been a missional community. Wherever Christians have gone, they've taken their faith with them and shared the good news about Jesus. But they not only spoke about it—they also lived it out in concrete ways. The reason is simple: it's a direct imitation of Jesus or a direct commission from Jesus. The mission of the church comes from Christ.

TALK ABOUT IT

Welcome to the seventh session of *The New Testament You Never Knew*. To get things started, discuss one of the following questions as a group:

- What was something you initially thought was relatively simple but you then discovered was far more complex than you dreamed?

—*or*—

- In what way would you describe the mission of the church? How do you feel the church is doing in fulfilling this mission as you understand it?

VIDEO TEACHING NOTES

Play the video segment for session seven. As you watch, use the space provided to collect your thoughts and make some notes about the New Testament that are new and fresh for you.

The Gospel in the New Testament

The gospel is foreshadowed in the Old Testament

The gospel is part of the kingdom of God

The gospel is about the status and story of Jesus

The gospel calls for faith and repentance

The gospel is about salvation

The Gospel

A summary of the gospel as presented in the New Testament would be something like this: it is the royal announcement that Jesus is the Messiah and Lord and, by his death and resurrection, God has won a victory over sin and death. By faith in Christ and turning away from our sin, we can receive the offer of salvation that God gives us in his Son, the risen Messiah.

The Message of the Early Church

The one true God sets people free from idols and false gods

God made the world and is in the business of remaking it

The Paradox of the Gospel

The gospel advances through suffering . . . but is unchained

The Church and Serving the Poor

Jesus' ministry of caring for the poor

The distinguishing marks of the early church

The Church and God's Kingdom

The whole of creation will one day be set free from its slavery

The church's mission of producing signs of new creation

God's Greater Kingdom Story

It is important for us to understand the gospel as part of God's greater kingdom story. Even in the Garden of Eden, we see God establishing his kingdom—his reign—over all creation. When sin enters, we see God giving a promise to his people that they will yet reign over the earth. The gospel is part of God's plan to repossess the world for himself and to put the world to right. Kingdom and gospel always go together.

GROUP DISCUSSION

Take a few minutes to discuss what you just watched and explore these concepts together.

1. In the ancient world, faith and religion permeated every aspect of a person's public and private activities. With this in mind, how would a person's life have radically changed if he or she decided to follow Jesus as their Savior? Why do you think this was seen as such a threat to the culture of the ancient world?

2. Read the following passages about the mission of the church and meaning of the gospel:

> Paul, a slave of King Jesus, called to be an apostle, set apart for God's good news, which he promised beforehand through his prophets in the sacred writings—the good news about his son, who was descended from David's seed in terms of flesh, and who was marked out powerfully as God's son in terms of the spirit of holiness by the resurrection of the dead: Jesus, the king, our Lord! (Romans 1:1–4).

> What I handed on to you at the beginning, you see, was what I received, namely this: "The Messiah died for our sins in accordance with the Bible; he was buried; he was raised on the third day in accordance with the Bible" (1 Corinthians 15:3–4).

> Remember Jesus the king, risen from the dead, from the seed of David, according to my gospel (2 Timothy 2:8).

According to these passages, what are some of the core beliefs and truths we need to understand if we are going to share the gospel with others? Why are these central to our faith and essential if we are going to stay on the mission of Jesus?

3. Read the following passage from John about the coming of God's kingdom:

> And I saw the holy city, the new Jerusalem, coming down out of heaven, from God, prepared like a bride dressed up for her husband. I heard a loud voice from the throne, and this is what it said: "Look! God has come to dwell with humans!

He will dwell with them, and they will be his people, and God himself will be with them and will be their God. He will wipe away every tear from their eyes. There will be no more death or mourning or weeping or pain anymore, since the first things have passed away." The one who sat on the throne said, "Look, I am making all things new" (Revelation 21:2–5).

How is the coming of the kingdom of God (both now and in the future) a central part of the message of the gospel? How can the confidence of knowing God's kingdom is here now and coming fully at the end of time help to propel us on the mission of Jesus?

4. The gospel is about the status and the story of Jesus—about who he is and not just what he does for us. How will our lives change if we decide to live as if Jesus is truly the leader of our lives? What tends to get in the way of leading this kind of life?

Don't Oversimplify the Gospel

We often settle for terse or simple statements about the gospel. We might say, "God loves you and has a good plan for your life." Maybe we try to dissect the gospel into a three-point argument like, "God is holy, people are sinful, and we need a mediator." These are true statements in their own way, but the gospel as presented in the New Testament is never put in such simple and short terms. There is more depth and nuance.

5. Read the following passages about the redeeming, justifying, cleansing, and saving work of Jesus:

> Grace to you and peace from God our father and Jesus the Messiah, our Lord, who gave himself for our sins, to rescue us from the present evil age, according to the will of God our father, to whom be glory to the ages of ages. Amen (Galatians 1:3–5).

> Let me explain it like this. Through the law I died to the law, so that I might live to God. I have been crucified with the Messiah. I am, however, alive—but it isn't me any longer; it's the Messiah who lives in me. And the life I do still live in the flesh, I live within the faithfulness of the son of God, who loved me and gave himself for me (Galatians 2:19–20).

> For this reason, Jesus is the mediator of the new covenant. The purpose was that those who are called should receive the promised inheritance of the age to come, since a death has occurred which provides redemption from transgressions committed under the first covenant (Hebrews 9:15).

> "The word is near you, in your mouth and in your heart" (that is, the word of faith which we proclaim); because if you profess with your mouth that Jesus is Lord, and believe in your heart that God raised him from the dead, you will be saved. Why? Because the way to covenant membership is by believing with the heart, and the way to salvation is by professing with the mouth. The Bible says, you see, "Everyone who believes in him will not be put to shame" (Romans 10:8–11).

The New Testament paints many pictures of what salvation in Christ looks like for a believer. What are some of the images and spiritual truths these passages paint for you?

6. Read the following account of Paul's teaching in Athens:

> So Paul stood up in the midst of the Areopagus.
>
> "Men of Athens," he said, "I see that you are in every way an extremely religious people. For as I was going along and looking at your objects of worship, I saw an altar with the inscription to an unknown god. Well: I'm here to tell you about what it is that you are worshipping in ignorance. The God who made the world and everything in it, the one who is Lord of heaven and earth, doesn't live in temples made by human hands. Nor does he need to be looked after by human hands, as though he lacked something, since he himself gives life and breath and all things to everyone. He made from one stock every race of humans to live on the whole face of the earth, allotting them their properly ordained times and the boundaries for their dwellings. The aim was that they would search for God, and perhaps reach out for him and find him. Indeed, he is actually not far from each one of us, for in him we live and move and exist; as also some of your own poets have put it, 'For we are his offspring.'
>
> "Well, then, if we really are God's offspring, we ought not to suppose that the divinity is like gold or silver or stone, formed by human skill and ingenuity. That was just ignorance; but the time for it has passed, and God has drawn a veil over it. Now, instead, he commands all people everywhere to repent, because he has established a day on which he intends to call the world to account with full and proper justice by a man whom he has appointed. God has given all people his pledge of this by raising this man from the dead" (Acts 17:22–31).

What did you learn about sharing the story of Jesus as you read this account? What is the heartbeat of Paul's message in this passage?

7. Read the following call to action from James' letter to the church:

> What use is it, my dear family, if someone says they have faith when they don't have works? Can faith save such a person? Supposing a brother or sister is without clothing, and is short even of daily food, and one of you says to them, "Go in peace; be warm, be full!"—but doesn't give them what their bodies need—what use is that? in the same way, faith, all by itself and without works, is dead (James 2:14–17).

How does a true understanding of the gospel and the mission of the church lead to compassionately caring for those in need? How does your church enter into ministry to the forgotten and marginalized? How can you be a greater part of this ministry?

8. What are some of the idols in our culture? How can we cast these down and lift up practices and attitudes that truly honor Jesus and reflect his presence in the world?

Every Generation Has Idols

Every culture generates its own idols. In the western world, we might say three big ones are Mammon (the god of money), Aphrodite (the god of sex), and Mars (the god of war). One of the tasks of the church today is to help Christians learn to worship the true God instead of idols. Instead of letting warlike thinking prevail, we should develop an attitude that says, "Blessed are the peacemakers." Instead of following whatever sexual energy demands, we ought to be sustaining healthy marriages. Instead of being consumed with money, we should grow in a desire to take care of the poorest of the poor and share what God has given us. These are just some of the ways we can worship the creator God and cast down the idols of today.

CLOSING PRAYER

Take time as a group to pray in some of the following directions . . .

- Thank God for loving you so much that he sent his only Son to suffer, bear your shame, take your sins, die, and rise again to give life to you.
- Lift up those you care about who do not know the good news of the gospel. Pray for their hearts to soften and be open to the good news of Christ. Ask God to give you courage to share the story of Jesus when the time is right.
- Ask God to give you a deeper and richer understanding of his mission and the greatness of the gospel.
- Ask the Spirit of God to challenge and convict you of the need to enter into a ministry of compassion and care for the hurting.
- Pray for God to show you any idols that exist in your life or are lurking in your heart. Repent of these and ask Jesus to always be enough for you.

Between-Sessions
Personal Study

Reflect on the content you've covered this week in *The New Testament You Never Knew* by engaging in any or all of the following between-sessions activities. The time you invest will be well spent, so let God use it to draw you closer to him. At your next meeting, share with your group any key points or insights that stood out to you as you spent this time with the Lord.

REFLECTION

In light of all you learned in this session, how would you describe the *gospel*?

In light of all you learned in this session, how would you describe the mission of the church?

What are idols you are tempted to hold in your heart and allow in your life? What can you do to cast these idols down and lift Jesus up?

Write out prayers for people in your life who need to understand the gospel and receive the grace of Jesus by faith.

STUDY

Commit to spending some time this week to read the following passages related to the mission of the church and the gospel. Write down any new insights you discover as you read.

Day 1: John 3–4

Insights you learned about missions and the gospel . . .

Day 2: Luke 15

Insights you learned about missions and the gospel . . .

Day 3: Acts 1

Insights you learned about missions and the gospel . . .

Day 4: Romans 1

Insights you learned about missions and the gospel . . . .

Day 5: 2 Corinthians 5

Insights you learned about missions and the gospel . . .

RESPONSE

Take time in the coming week to commit these following passages to memory. Let the message of the gospel of Jesus fill your heart and mind, and be on your lips!

> I'm not ashamed of the good news; it's God's power, bringing salvation to everyone who believers—to the Jew first, and also, equally, to the Greek. This is because God's covenant justice is unveiled in it, from faithfulness to faithfulness. As it says in the Bible, "the just shall live by faith" (Romans 1:16–17).

> What I handed on to you at the beginning, you see, was what I received, namely this: "The Messiah died for our sins in accordance with the Bible; he was buried; he was raised on the third day in accordance with the Bible" (1 Corinthians 15:3–4).

> Remember Jesus the king, risen from the dead, from the seed of David, according to my gospel (2 Timothy 2:8).

APPLICATION

Consider two practical ways you can show care and compassion in the next thirty days for those who are hurting, outcast, and forgotten. Some ideas include (1) learning what your church does to help those in need (and then getting involved), (2) partnering with a local mission agency in your area, or (3) even starting your own compassion ministry. As you serve, take notes on how you feel the presence of Jesus, how God impacts the lives of those you serve, and how the Holy Spirit grows your faith and expands your heart to make it more like the heart of Jesus.

Idea #1:

What you will do to act on the idea . . .

Idea #2:

What you will do to act on the idea . . .

FOR NEXT WEEK

Use the space below to write any key insights or questions from your personal study that you want to discuss at the next group meeting.

THE CREATION OF THE NEW TESTAMENT

The Bible didn't fall out of the sky, bound in
leather, with the words of Jesus colored in red.
The New Testament in particular came to us
through a particular process by which its text was
transmitted, recorded, and formally canonized over
time. Eventually, it was translated into thousands
of languages around the world. While there are
other writings out there, the basic consensus of the
church has been that the twenty-seven books that
make up our New Testament are the authorized
list of sacred writings for the Christian church.

MICHAEL F. BIRD

INTRODUCTION

Have you ever put together a large and complex jigsaw puzzle? It is a fascinating process. When you buy the puzzle, it comes in a box with a picture of the final product on the font. A beautiful seascape, a dog with puppies, a snow-covered country scene, or some other image you will be piecing together for hours, days, or even weeks.

When you first look at the picture, it might appear the puzzle will be simple to put together. But then you open the box and pour out the pieces on a tabletop . . . and you realize this will take some effort. This is where the fun begins.

Everyone has his or her own approach and personal puzzle-building style. A common method is to first turn over all the pieces so you can see the picture side and not the cardboard side. You then find the corners and edges and then organize the pieces by color or common elements found in the picture.

Once these steps are complete, you begin putting the edge together . . . and maybe complete the entire frame of the picture with the edges and corners all in place. You then start building the easily identifiable parts of the picture, fill in the tough parts, and search on the floor for the one or two pieces that are missing. At some point, you pop in the final piece and look at the same picture that was on the box before you started.

It is a truly fascinating process.

When God gave people his Word, the Bible, he did not give them the finished puzzle. In a sense, he gave them the box filled with so many pieces that it took *centuries* for them to put it together. It wasn't just one person who worked on this puzzle, but countless individuals from a rich mix of times, places, backgrounds, cultures, and languages. It was not an exclusively human process, but God guided each step of the way . . . and he is the One who made all the pieces.

Although the puzzle that is the Bible is complete today, God releases fresh inspiration, hope, conviction, truth, and power to each new generation who reads it. The same Spirit who guided the process of putting the Bible together also guides us as we read it—whether that is on our own, with family and friends, or in community among God's people.

The words and content of the Bible are divine and powerful, for God breathed them through the centuries. The message of the Bible is transformational, for the Spirit of God continues to teach his people. And the process of the Bible being given to us is dynamic, for as each piece was put in place, a divine and human partnership happened.

That is way more exciting than a finished puzzle being delivered from heaven!

TALK ABOUT IT

Welcome to the final session of *The New Testament You Never Knew*. To get things started, discuss one of the following questions as a group:

- When was the first time you held a Bible, had the Bible read to you, or got your own copy? What do you recall thinking about this book?

—*or*—

- When someone says, "The Bible is the Word of God," what do you think that means? How was God involved in forming and giving the Bible to us?

Bible Translation Is Not New

The Old Testament was translated into Greek between the third and first centuries BC, to make it accessible to those who didn't know the original Aramaic or Hebrew. The Bible has been translated into language after language ever since. It is not the sort of book one can glance at for a few minutes, get the right answers, and stop thinking about it. The Bible challenges each generation to think afresh. The Bible is the book that fuels and informs the mission of the church.

VIDEO TEACHING NOTES

Play the video segment for session eight. As you watch, use the space provided to collect your thoughts and make some notes about the New Testament that are new and fresh for you.

Reliability of the New Testament Texts

The number of manuscripts of the New Testament available to us

The macro-level stability and continuity of the text over the ages

Form of the New Testament Texts

Scrolls and early books (codices)

The desire to have the Gospels bound together

Textual Variances

There are thousands of ancient texts of the New Testament, and within these manuscripts are thousands of small variations. Usually, these are just differences in wording or spelling. We do find occasions where a cheeky scribe has done something a bit peculiar, but for the most part the manuscripts show a great degree of stability and sameness. Also, because we have ancient texts of the Bible not just in Greek and Latin but also in Arminian, Syriac, and Arabic, we can compare these manuscripts together to see how the New Testament has been translated over the ages.

Early Translations of the Bible

The Greek New Testament and Latin Vulgate

Textus Receptus (the "received text")

Developments in translations in the nineteenth century

English Translations of the Bible

Tyndale's desire to translate the Bible into the language of the ordinary people

Tyndale's flight from England and eventual execution

The Passion of William Tyndale

William Tyndale, like others in England in the early sixteenth century, was fed up with the way the church failed to get the teaching of the Bible into the hearts and minds of ordinary people. At the time, the Bible was only read in Latin. Most people of the day didn't understand Latin, so the clergy would tell them what the passage meant. Tyndale felt this wasn't good enough, so he risked his life to translate the Bible into a language the people could understand.

The New Testament Canon

False understandings of how the books of the Bible were chosen

Canonization was a gradual process achieved over time

GROUP DISCUSSION

Take a few minutes to discuss what you just watched and explore these concepts together.

1. What is something new or surprising you learned from the teaching about the process God used to form the New Testament? How will this information affect the way you see the Bible and understand the One who gave us his Word?

2. Read the following passages about the Bible:

> Oh, how I love your law!
>> It is my meditation all day long.
> Your commandment makes me wiser than my enemies,
>> for it is always with me.
> I have more understanding than all my teachers,
>> for your decrees are my meditation.
> I understand more than the aged,
>> for I keep your precepts.
> I hold back my feet from every evil way,
>> in order to keep your word.
> I do not turn away from your ordinances,
>> for you have taught me.
> How sweet are your words to my taste,
>> sweeter than honey to my mouth!
> Through your precepts I get understanding;
>> therefore I hate every false way.
> Your word is a lamp to my feet
>> and a light to my path (Psalm 119:97–105).

"You study the Bible," Jesus continued, "because you suppose that you'll discover the life of God's coming age in it. In fact, it's the Bible which gives evidence about me!" (John 5:39).

But you, on the other hand, must stand firm in the things you learned and believed. You know who it was you received them from, and how from childhood you have known the holy writings which have the power to make you wise for salvation through faith in King Jesus. All scripture is breathed by God, and it is useful for teaching, for rebuke, for improvement, for training in righteousness, so that people who belong to God may be complete, fitted out and ready for every good work (2 Timothy 3:14–17).

And we have the prophetic word made more certain. You will do well to hold on to this, as to a lamp shining in a dark place, until the day dawns and the morning star shines in your hearts. You must know this first of all, that no scriptural prophecy is a matter of one's own interpretation. No prophecy, you see, ever came by human will. Rather, people were moved by the holy spirit, and spoke from God (2 Peter 1:19–21).

How have you experienced the Bible serving as a light for your path? How has the Bible taught you or rebuked you? How have you grown in wisdom as you have read and followed the teachings in the Bible?

3. It is clear the core messages of the Bible have not been compromised over time, but there are "variations" between some of the ancient manuscripts. Do you believe this undermines the truth and authority of the Bible? Or is the high level of agreement a testimony to God's protection of the biblical text? Explain your answer.

4. Some people approach the Bible with a mindset that throws the baby out with the bathwater. If there is one disagreement between manuscripts, they reject the whole Bible. Why is this way of looking at the Bible dangerous? Why is it important to recognize the divine God used human beings in writing and shaping of the Bible?

Myths About the Formation of the Bible

There are many wrong theories about how the books of the Bible were chosen. One is that the Bible was manufactured by the Roman emperor Constantine during the fourth century AD and then imposed on the church. Another is that early church leaders traveled with some kind of "inspiration-o-meter" looking for texts that were written by the apostles and thus inspired. Many people have come up with other theories to debunk the value and authority of the Bible. But the truth is it was a long process, done over time in community, and led by the Holy Spirit.

5. How are you inspired by the story of William Tyndale and his willingness to give his life to translate the Bible into the language of the ordinary people? What can you do to help the people in your life discover, read, and learn from the Bible?

2. What are some of the potential benefits of reading the Bible in large sections (reading a number of chapters at one time)? What are some of the values of reading shorter portions of the Bible (a chapter or less) and meditating on the text, reflecting on its meaning, and infusing it in your soul and life? How can these two kinds of Bible reading supplement and strengthen each other?

3. Read the following account of Mary's humble obedience:

> "The holy spirit will come upon you," replied the angel, "and the power of the Most High will overshadow you. For that reason the Holy One who is born from you will be called God's son.
>
> "Let me tell you this, too: your cousin Elizabeth, in her old age, has also conceived a son. This is the sixth month for her, a woman who people used to say was barren. With God, you see, nothing is impossible."
>
> "Here I am," said Mary; "I'm the Lord's servant-girl. Let it happen to me as you've said." Then the angel left her (Luke 1:35–38).

Mary sets a beautiful example in this passage of surrender to the will of God. How would your reading and study of the Bible change if you approached it with a heart like Mary? How can you live with greater surrender to what God teaches in the Bible?

4. Read this challenging exhortation from James:

> But be people who do the word, not merely people who hear it and deceive themselves. Someone who hears the word but doesn't do it, you see, is like a man who looks at his natural face in a mirror. He notices himself, but then he goes away and quickly forgets what he looked like. But the person who looks into the perfect law of freedom, and goes on with it, not being a hearer who forgets but a doer who does the deed—such a person is blessed in their doing (James 1:22–25).

What is one biblical lesson you are trying to follow but are finding challenging? What action do you feel God wants you to take? How can your group members pray for you, cheer you on, and help you live in greater obedience to Christ?

A Bible-Reading Legacy

It is important for us to remember that we walk in a rich tradition of Bible reading and interpretation. Our brothers and sisters from previous generations loved the Bible and learned from God's wisdom in the Scriptures. There are countless people who have read it before us and learned from God, and what they discovered should stimulate us to do for our generation what they did for theirs. Every new generation should learn from the past and share what they discover with the next generation.

CLOSING PRAYER

Take time as a group to pray in some of the following directions . . .

- Thank God for the beautiful and mysterious way he formed and brought the Bible together in partnership with real people over the centuries.
- Thank God for the people who have taught you to know and love the Bible.
- Pray for group members who want to grow in knowing and following the teaching of the Bible. Ask the Spirit of God to give them power and discipline to surrender their lives to his will.
- Ask God to give you growing assurance that the Bible is true and powerful to guide your life.
- Thank God for those faithful people who have gone before you and translated the Bible, copied manuscripts, and counted the cost as they partnered with God to bring you his Word.

Final Personal Study

Reflect on the content you've covered this week in *The New Testament You Never Knew* by engaging in any or all of the following personal study activities. The time you invest will be well spent, so let God use it to draw you closer to him. Be sure to share with your group leader or group members in the upcoming weeks any key points or insights that stood out to you.

REFLECTION

What did you learn about the process of the Bible coming into existence that surprised you? What new insight did that provide for you?

How did God work in partnership with people throughout the centuries to bring you the Bible? How does this make the Bible even more rich, beautiful, and accessible?

What steps can you take to read the Bible for all it is worth?

Write down a prayer for those in your life who have doubts or questions about Jesus or the Bible. Ask God to open their eyes to the truth of his Word and give them his wisdom.

STUDY

Psalm 119 is the longest chapter of the Bible. The core focus of this amazing psalm is the Bible. The psalmist uses terms like *precepts*, *commands*, *laws*, *decrees*, *word*, and more . . . but they all point to the Scriptures. Interestingly, each section of this psalm begins with a letter from the Hebrew alphabet. In a sense, it is a description of God's Word from *A* to *Z*! Each day this week, read a portion of this psalm (at least twice) and then reflect on what you learned about God's Word and how it should impact your life.

Day 1: Psalm 119:1–32

What you learned about God's Word and how it should impact your life . . .

Day 2: Psalm 119:33–72

What you learned about God's Word and how it should impact your life . . .

Day 3: Psalm 119:73–104

What you learned about God's Word and how it should impact your life . . .

Day 4: Psalm 119:105–144

What you learned about God's Word and how it should impact your life . . .

Day 5: Psalm 119:145–176

What you learned about God's Word and how it should impact your life . . .

RESPONSE AND APPLICATION

As you close this study on *The New Testament You Never Knew*, consider taking up the challenge of reading the *entire* Bible over the course of the next year. There are all sorts of reading plans and Bible apps available that can help you put together a plan. Just do a search for "one year Bible reading" or "plan for reading the Bible in one year."

Purchase a journal and write down at least one lesson you learn from your reading per week. If you don't like writing notes out by hand, start a file in your computer or make a note on your phone. If you are not a big reader, consider listening to the whole Bible in the course of the year. Most Bible apps have a listening feature available that you can use.

Along with this macro-reading, consider memorizing one verse each week. As you do your weekly reading, look for a verse that pops out at you and then commit to memorizing it over the course of the coming seven days. By the end of the year, you will have read or listened to the whole Bible and memorized fifty-two verses that impacted your life and took you deeper in faith. It will be a macro and micro year of the Bible!

LEADER'S GUIDE
FOR SMALL GROUPS

Thank you for your willingness to lead a group through *The New Testament You Never Knew*. What you have chosen to do is important, and much good fruit can come from studies like this. The rewards of being a leader are different from those of participating, and we hope that as you lead you will find your own walk with Jesus deepened by this experience.

The New Testament You Never Knew is an eight-session study built around video content and small-group interaction. As the group leader, imagine yourself as the host of a party. Your job is to take care of your guests by managing all the behind-the-scenes details so that as your guests arrive, they can focus on each other and on interaction around the topic.

As the group leader, your role is not to answer all the questions or reteach the content—the video and study guide will do most of that work. Your job is to guide the experience and cultivate your small group into a kind of teaching community. This will make it a place for members to process, question, and reflect—not receive more instruction.

There are several elements in this leader's guide that will help you as you structure your study and reflection time, so be sure to follow along and take advantage of each one.

BEFORE YOU BEGIN

Before your first meeting, make sure the group members have a copy of this study guide so they can follow along and have their answers written out ahead of time. Alternately, you can hand out the study guides at your first meeting and give the group members some time to look over the material and ask any preliminary questions. During your first meeting, be sure to send a sheet around the room and have the members write down their name, phone number, and/or email address so you can keep in touch with them during the week.

Generally, the ideal size for a group is between eight to ten people, which ensures everyone will have enough time to participate in discussions. If you have more people, you might want to break up the main group into smaller subgroups. Encourage those who show up at the first meeting to commit to attending for the duration of the study, as this will help the group members get to know each other, create stability for the group, and help you know how to prepare each week.

Each of the sessions begins with an opening reflection. The two questions that follow in the "Talk About It" section serve as an icebreaker to get the group members thinking about the topic at hand. Some people may want to tell a long story in response to one of these questions, but the goal is to keep the answers brief. Ideally, you want everyone in the group to get a chance to answer, so try to keep the responses to a minute or less. If you have talkative group members, say up front that everyone needs to limit the answer to one minute.

Give the group members a chance to answer, but tell them to feel free to pass if they wish. With the rest of the study, it's generally not a good idea to have everyone answer every question—a free-flowing discussion is more desirable. But with the opening icebreaker question, you can go around the circle. Encourage shy people to share, but don't force them.

Before your first meeting, let the group know each session contains four between-sessions activities (titled Reflection, Study, Response, and Application) they can complete during the week. While this is an optional exercise, it will help them cement the concepts presented during the group time and encourage them to spend time each day in God's Word. Also invite them to bring any questions and insights they uncovered while reading to your next meeting, especially if they had a breakthrough moment or didn't understand something.

WEEKLY PREPARATION

As the leader, there are a few things you should do to prepare for each meeting:

- *Read through the session.* This will help you to become familiar with the content and know how to structure the discussion times.
- *Decide which questions you definitely want to discuss.* Based on the length of the group discussion, you may not be able to get through all of the Bible study and group discussion questions, so choose four to five questions that you definitely want to cover.
- *Be familiar with the questions you want to discuss.* When the group meets you'll be watching the clock, so you want to make sure you are familiar with the questions you have selected. In this way, you'll ensure you have the material more deeply in your mind than your group members.
- *Pray for your group.* Pray for your group members throughout the week and ask God to lead them as they study his Word.
- *Bring extra supplies to your meeting.* The members should bring their own pens for writing notes, but it's a good idea to have extras available for those who forget. You may also want to bring paper and additional Bibles.

Note that in many cases there will be no one "right" answer to the question. Answers will vary, especially when the group members are being asked to share their personal experiences.

STRUCTURING THE DISCUSSION TIME

You will need to determine with your group how long you want to meet each week so you can plan your time accordingly. For this study, you will likely want to meet for either 90 or 120 minutes to cover the content, so you could use one of the following schedules:

Section	90 Minutes	120 Minutes
Welcome (members arrive and get settled)	10 minutes	15 minutes
Talk About It (discuss one of the two opening questions for the session)	10 minutes	15 minutes
Video (watch the teaching material together and take notes)	25 minutes	25 minutes
Discussion (discuss the Bible study questions you selected ahead of time)	35 minutes	50 minutes
Prayer/Closing (pray together as a group and dismiss)	10 minutes	15 minutes

As the group leader, it is up to you to keep track of the time and keep things moving along according to your schedule. You might want to set a timer for each segment so both you and the group members know when your time is up. (Note there are some good phone apps for timers that play a gentle chime or other pleasant sound instead of a disruptive noise.)

Don't be concerned if the group members are quiet or slow to share. People are often quiet when they are pulling together their ideas, and this might be a new experience for them. Just ask a question and let it hang in the air until someone shares. You can then say, "Thank you. What about others? What came to you when you watched that portion of the video?"

GROUP DYNAMICS

Leading a group through *The New Testament You Never Knew* will prove to be highly rewarding both to you and your group members. However, this doesn't mean you will not encounter any challenges along the way! Discussions can get off track. Group members may not be sensitive to the needs and ideas of others. Some might worry they will be expected to talk about matters that make them feel awkward. Others may express comments that result in disagreements. To help ease this strain on you and the group, consider the following ground rules:

- When someone raises a question or comment that is off the main topic, suggest you deal with it another time, or, if you feel led to go in that direction, let the group know you will be spending some time discussing it.

- If someone asks a question you don't know how to answer, admit it and move on. At your discretion, feel free to invite group members to comment on questions that call for personal experience.
- If you find one or two people are dominating the discussion time, direct a few questions to others in the group. Outside the main group time, ask the more dominating members to help you draw out the quieter ones. Work to make them a part of the solution instead of the problem.
- When a disagreement occurs, encourage the group members to process the matter in love. Encourage those on opposite sides to restate what they heard the other side say about the matter, and then invite each side to evaluate if that perception is accurate. Lead the group in examining other Scriptures related to the topic and look for common ground.

When any of these issues arise, encourage your group members to follow these words from the Bible: "Love one another" (John 13:34), "If it's possible, as far as you can, live at peace with all people" (Romans 12:18), and, "Every person should be quick to hear, slow to speak, slow to anger" (James 1:19). This will make your group time more rewarding and beneficial for everyone who attends.

Thank you again for your willingness to lead your group. May God reward your efforts and dedication and make your time together in *The New Testament You Never Knew* fruitful for his kingdom.